Historic
BLACK NEIGHBORHOODS
of
RALEIGH

Historic
BLACK NEIGHBORHOODS
of
RALEIGH

Carmen Wimberley Cauthen

THE
History
PRESS

Published by The History Press
Charleston, SC
www.historypress.com

Manufactured in the United States

ISBN 9781467150880

Library of Congress Control Number: 2022944981

To all those who treasure the truth of history.

To my ancestors who told us the stories and wanted us to know the truth of our heritage. To my children who understand that history and legacy are important.

The Winns, Gradys, Wimberleys and Peeles.
(The Grady Girls in particular.)

CONTENTS

Acknowledgements   9
Preface   11
Introduction   13

PART I. IMPLICATIONS OF SLAVERY ON NEIGHBORHOODS   **15**
Reconstruction after the Civil War   17
Lunsford Lane   19

PART II. LEGACY AFTER THE CIVIL WAR   **23**
General Information   25
Black Church Beginnings   30
Businesses   33
Freedmen's Bureau   52
Education and Raleigh's Black Schools   54
Richard B. Harrison Library   66
Fire Companies   69
Recreation   72
Politics   80

PART III. NEIGHBORHOODS   **91**
Oberlin Village (Free People)   93
Method   103
Lincolnville   112

Brooklyn   118
Cannon Lands/Hayti/Manly's Homestead   119
Hungry Neck   126
St. Petersburg   128
Cotton Place/Idlewild   129
College Park   146
Smoky Hollow   148
Old Fairgrounds   157
Smith-Haywood   161
Watson's Addition   165
South Park/East Raleigh   174
Wilmington-Blount   182

**PART IV. POST–WORLD WAR II NEIGHBORHOODS/NATIONAL
HISTORIC REGISTER**   **205**
Battery Heights   207
Rochester Heights   215
Madonna Acres   222

Conclusion   227
Bibliography   229
Index   235
About the Author   255

ACKNOWLEDGEMENTS

Thank you, Lord, for preparing me for this purpose. It has been a lifelong journey, and I didn't realize that this was the path I was headed on. Who knew that reading autobiographies growing up, writing the *House Journal* and watching history being made on a daily basis and then being able to categorize and index it would have led to this end.

This would not have been possible without the help of folks at the Olivia Raney Public Library who helped me find things that I didn't know I was looking for; folks at the State Library in the book and photo divisions; my sweet daughter, who took the photographs for me; my teachers from long ago who taught me how to research and use index cards to write with (only for old schoolers); my friends who encouraged me and chimed in with stories of their own, documents and their family knowledge; the students and teachers who allowed me to share stories with them during tours and talks; the members of the Wake County Housing Justice Coalition who originally asked me to tell the story of affordable housing that led down this path; and those who trust in the truth and aren't afraid to find out where it leads.

Know that there is so much more to uncover and share.

PREFACE

R aleigh, North Carolina's African American history is not complex. It is the story of a people who—despite slavery—desired to learn, grow and be on par with and treated just as any other humans.

The recognition for most African Americans, coloreds, Blacks, Negroes, people of color (and all terms will be used interchangeably throughout the book) was and is that education is a must—a necessity—in order to move forward, both individually and as a people. If the ability to read and write is held back, it is impossible for a race or culture to move forward and compete in any manner. Raleigh, North Carolina, was then extremely fortunate to have access to the education provided by Shaw Institute (University) and St. Augustine's Institute (University) and to have neighborhoods that were built up around both institutions.

To understand this is to begin to grasp the fundamentals of neighborhood building in the African American communities in Raleigh, from the 1860s until today.

INTRODUCTION

I n order to talk about the African American neighborhoods in Raleigh, North Carolina, it is important to discuss the implications of slavery, the Civil War and its legacy for plantation life and its end, as well as the changes that occurred during Reconstruction (1863–90) with the aid of the Freedmen's Bureau in the city and the role of economics and business during the post–World War II era.

This book will look at politics, institutions, people and the roles they all played in growing the city of Raleigh's neighborhoods through the 1970s. It is impossible to share any of the history without going into detail on the policy of the day.

Information shared is interspersed around each neighborhood—from Oberlin Village (begun in 1858), a village created by free men, to the freedman's villages outside the city proper, such as Masonville (now known as Method) and Lincolnville (no longer existing). Freedman's villages more readily part of the city or created from plantations include Hungry Neck, St. Petersburg, Cotton Place, Idlewild, Old Fairgrounds, Hayti, Cannon Lands, Manly's Homestead, Smith-Haywood and Watson's Addition. Brooklyn, Smoky Hollow, South Park and Wilmington-Blount are four other areas that will be briefly mentioned, as they played a role in the neighborhood growth. (South Park–East Raleigh is a National Historic Register neighborhood.)

Finally, the post–World War II National Historic Register neighborhoods of Rochester Heights, Battery Heights and Madonna Acres will be discussed.

Part I

IMPLICATIONS OF SLAVERY ON NEIGHBORHOODS

The city of Raleigh was established in 1792 as the capital of the state of North Carolina, before the Civil War and the end of slavery. The city was platted after the purchase of the land from Joel Lane. It was planned with the state capital set in the center and then spread out in a one-mile square to the east, west, north and south.

Various plantations or estates filled the area, although originally there were very few large slaveholding acreages. As the city grew, so did the size of the estates and plantations. While many farm estates had families that were able to do all of the work, they were generally on the outskirts of the city, in the county. The family homes and estates that were within the city boundaries generally had slaves who lived and worked both inside and outside the home.

Several of the plantations and estates that will forever be part of the history of the African American neighborhoods in Raleigh include the lands of Governor Charles Manly; Willie Jones; the Mordecai estate of Duncan Cameron; the Daniel M. Barringer estate; Governor Worth's estate; the M.A. Bledsoe Plantation; Colonel Jonathan McGee Heck's estate; and the Watson family's estate. The legacy of the Civil War hastened the end of these large estates.

1807 CENSUS

Raleigh City Wards	Free Blacks	Slaves	Whites
East	28	111	197
Middle	3	107	140
West	2	52	86
Totals	33	270	423

RECONSTRUCTION
AFTER THE CIVIL WAR

T o completely understand why we talk about Reconstruction, we must understand how the Civil War tore the economic fabric of the South. In order to see that, we must recognize that the southern economy was based totally on slavery or free labor. While there were costs of doing business, the cost of labor was never added into the profit margin.

The fact that slavery ended meant that plantations, whether large or small, could no longer be run at the same profit margin. And because the South lost the war, there was no more legal free labor. Also, because of the cost of the war, most of the plantations could no longer operate effectively.

Some of the federal Works Progress Administration (WPA) slave narratives talk about how slaves and slave owners found out that slaves had been emancipated. Charity Austin, who lived on South Bloodworth Street, said that "the boss told them that Abraham Lincoln was dead, and they were still slaves." The master bought black cloth, and the slaves had to wear mourning. They were required to remain as slaves for another year. It wasn't until someone from the Freedmen's Bureau found out that the overseer had killed someone that they were told they were free.

Viney Baker, of South Harrington Street, said that her mother was sold while she slept in the bed beside her one night. She received regular beatings before and after slavery ended. The soldiers who came didn't assure them of their freedom, and the owner in Durham County didn't acknowledge their freedom. Her mother returned and got her when she was around twelve years old.

While in theory, one would suppose that most slaves did not understand government, it is obvious that some did. Many of the newly freed slaves were able to take the trades they performed on the plantation and create jobs or businesses for themselves outside that economic situation.

In 1860, Blacks composed 20 to 40 percent of the population of the typical southern city. Raleigh was no different. Slaves were regularly hired out as railroad laborers and servants to people other than their owners for pay. The owners would allow them to keep a portion of the funds that they received for the work. Slaves helped to build the state capitol building, and many may have lived outside of their slave masters' quarters in order to do this. This is how people like Lunsford Lane were able to save money and purchase their freedom and the freedom of their family members.

LUNSFORD LANE

Lunsford Lane was born a slave on May 30, 1803. He was the only child of house slaves, Edward and Clarissa Lane, of the Sherwood Haywood family. His father, Edward, was listed in Joel Lane's 1795 will as "young Ned," and he was left to Joel's wife, Mary. He remained on the Lane estate for four years after her death until he was sold to John Haywood of Haywood Hall. The last name of Lane was taken from the Joel Lane family by Lunsford's parents. While Lunsford Lane lived with a paternalistic master, he still feared being sold away from his parents.

He began to learn to be an entrepreneur after selling a basket of peaches that had been given to him by his father. After earning that money, he began to save tips from house guests who visited the Haywood household. He chopped and sold wood. He purchased supplies for the Haywood family and learned to buy in quantity when prices were low so that he could save money. He would also buy goods for himself at a bargain, store the items and sell them when prices rose.

Lane carved pipes and sold them. His father helped him to develop a specially flavored tobacco, which he sold in Raleigh to members of the state legislature. As he prospered, he hired agents to sell his tobacco in Fayetteville, Salisbury and Chapel Hill. He worked as a slave by day and worked for-profit at night. The tobacco that he sold was branded the Edward and Lunsford Lane tobacco.

He says that he was obsessed with buying his freedom and also was obsessed with making the money to do so. He married Martha Curtis. She had originally been owned by the Boylan family, who sold her to Raleigh merchant Benjamin B. Smith. After she and Lunsford were married, her owner refused to provide food and clothing for her or their six children because Lane's income was sufficient to meet their needs. This meant Lane had to make even more money to save to purchase the family's freedom.

In 1835, Lane purchased his freedom for $1,000. He made arrangements to purchase his family for $2,500. He also arranged for his wife's owner to "buy" him and then take him to New York. Although he had paid the required purchase price for himself, the courts of North Carolina said he had not earned his freedom meritoriously, so he was still considered a slave. (In this case, "meritorious services must consist in more than mere general performance of duty," according to North Carolina Session Laws of 1830, Chapter 9, Section 4.)

After going to New York, Lane petitioned the courts for freeman status, which he received. In order to continue raising funds, he told the story of his life at antislavery meetings. He returned to North Carolina and lived in a house that he had earlier purchased in Raleigh while still enslaved. His family was allowed to live with him. During this period, he worked for Governor Edward B. Dudley by keeping order in his office, running errands and making deliveries.

Because he had lived in New York temporarily while petitioning for freeman status, Lane became victim of a statute that forbade free Blacks from another state staying in North Carolina for more than twenty days. In 1840, the secretary to the governor wrote a letter of request to extend the time Lane was able to stay in North Carolina, but he was required to leave in 1841. This was considered a legal matter, so the request was sent to court. The prosecutor was not prepared to handle the case, so it was postponed for three months. During this time, Lane was able to negotiate a petition of relief that was signed by twenty-five men of good reputation. This was sent to the legislature as evidence of his strengths as a respectable, hardworking man. This residency extension fight took three years from the time of recommendation until the time of petition and the court proceedings. Because he was colored, he was not allowed in the Senate chamber during the arguments. The request was denied, and he was banished from the state.

By 1842, Lane had raised enough funds to return to Raleigh to secure the freedom of his wife and children. On his return, he was arrested for having delivered abolitionist lectures in the North. These charges were dropped. It is believed that Lane's economic success angered whites because the belief of white racial superiority didn't allow for Black financial success.

While Lane was being escorted back to the jail for safety reasons, a mob captured him with the intention of hanging him but instead tarred and feathered him. Some of the mob members included former friends who then helped him to escape. After Lane quickly gathered his family, they were barely able to catch a train and go free. Lane's mother had received her freedom by manumission and traveled with them. His father was later released.

In 1842, Lane wrote his autobiography, titled *The Narrative of Lunsford Lane, Formerly of Raleigh North Carolina, Embracing an Account of His Early Life, the Redemption by Purchase of Himself and Family from Slavery and His Banishment from the Place of His Birth for the Crime of Wearing a Colored Skin*. Lane's autobiography was sold throughout America and England. He became an active member of the American Anti-Slavery Society, which was founded in 1833 and led by William Lloyd Garrison.

The family lived in the northern cities of Philadelphia, New York, Boston, Worcester and Oberlin. He was named as one of the speakers at the 1848 Massachusetts State Anniversary. He moved with his wife to Cambridge, Massachusetts, where their seventh child was born. According to records, he had practiced as a physician at some point in Raleigh, and after his arrival in the Massachusetts area, he marketed herbal medicines and was also listed as a physician in the 1870 census. He was also listed as a steward at Wellington Hospital. Lunsford Lane died in Manhattan, New York, on June 27, 1879.

Free Blacks were considered peculiar. Their status was not slave but also not really free. In the 1820s and after the Nat Turner uprising in 1831, the State of North Carolina passed laws that "stripped free blacks of the vote, of the right to preach, the right to carry firearms, to marry white or slaves, or to transact business with slaves." The laws also opposed formal education of free Blacks.

Unless a free Black person was educated, he was only able to work menial or low-paying jobs. These were considered "Negro jobs." This only increased after the Civil War. The jobs were unskilled mill or railroad labor, domestic service or road gang employment. Sometimes they could earn enough money to buy their freedom, but this took diligence, apprenticeships and luck. Formerly enslaved people who had the following types of training were able to gain middle-class status after slavery: barbers, draymen, carpenters, brick masons, stonecutters and harness makers.

OCCUPATIONS

barbers
sextons
carpenter
hairdressers
workmen
bank servant
boarding housekeepers
policemen
newspaper press
lodging housekeepers
detectives
tinner
stationary engineers
waiters and waitresses
plasterer

firemen
teachers
stewards
hotel keepers
clergymen
cooks
janitors
doctors
cemetery sexton
laborers
pharmacist
seamstress
launderers and
    laundresses
real estate

landscape gardener
nurses
soft drink supplier
well digger
midwives
grocers
miller
restaurant owners
blacksmith
coppersmith
saloonkeepers
shoemaker
servants
mechanics

tinner (makes things of light metals)
coppersmith (makes things of copper)
blacksmith (makes and repairs things made of iron, using heat and cold
    and anvil)

Part II

LEGACY AFTER THE CIVIL WAR

After the surrender of both the overall Confederacy and the city of Raleigh, life was very different for whites, former slaves and those who had already been free. Although President Lincoln had given notice of his intent to free the slaves in a September 22, 1862 proclamation and the actual proclamation of freedom on January 1, 1863, slaves in the South were not freed until the end of the war, around the end of 1865. On April 14 and 15, 1865, Union armies entered the capital city to occupy it after surrender by both Governor Vance and Mayor William H. Harrison.

We are told by Robert Hinton's statement from the WPA slave narratives that the marching soldiers included "colored folks soldiers in blue clothes too. In de mornin' white soldiers, in de evenin' [afternoon] colored soldiers." (This was General Charles Paine's Third Division of the Tenth Corps, nine regiments of U.S. Colored Troops.) Returning soldiers and those slaves who had been sent to serve with their masters or masters' families returned morally defeated, emaciated from lack of food and water, "ragged, dirty, and pale to find their farms stripped, plantations overgrown with weeds, their cotton destroyed, and their laborers disbanded," according to Union General O.O. Howard, who would become head of the Freedmen's Bureau.

As part of the Reconstruction government on May 29, 1865, President Johnson appointed William Woods Holden as the provisional governor of North Carolina. In order to qualify as a delegate for the Constitutional Convention, each nominated delegate had to take an amnesty oath. As part of Reconstruction in the Raleigh municipal government, Governor Holden appointed two Negroes to the City Board of Commissioners in 1868.

They were State Representative James H. Harris of the Western Ward and Hardy Lockhart of the Eastern Ward. The city police appointments included a Negro assistant to the police chief. Three colored policemen were also appointed. They were Wesley or Willie Hunter, Simon Craven and Robert Crosson.

GENERAL INFORMATION

The antebellum residential area of Raleigh was in the downtown area. There were thirty blocks, and the boundaries were Davie Street to the south; South Street to the north; East and West Streets. Fayetteville Street was the dividing line. This was a prestigious address, and it divided the city into southwest and southeast quadrants.

In 1857, the city annexed property one mile in each direction from the capital. Before the 1857 annexation, racially segregated areas were called the suburbs. Enslaved Blacks lived everywhere. Residential patterns suggest that Blacks were interspersed in the city but that free Blacks tended to live among each other. There was racial and economic segregation. On the eve of the Civil War, there were 152 white families who owned slaves who resided in the main house. They lived in separate wings, basements, upper stories and detached back dwellings.

The 1860 census records free Blacks living as servants and laborers and boarding in fifty-five white households. There were integrated blocks of skilled workers and laborers. That was commonplace. Railroad-related industries had working-class white families frequently living nearby. Black families also lived in those same areas. Free Blacks lived in small enclaves especially in the southern periphery, where the railroad tracks crossed Fayetteville Street. In northwest Raleigh, free Blacks lived in low-lying terrain near the railroad repair shops.

The southeast quadrant of Raleigh was built around Second Baptist Church at the corner of Blount and Cabarrus Streets, which was built in

1866. It is now Tupper Memorial Baptist Church. This was the church that Raleigh Institute, now Shaw University, was started in. Other institutions that brought Blacks to southeast Raleigh included the colored Department of the Deaf, Dumb and Blind Institute (or Asylum) that was on South Bloodworth Street.

The southwest quadrant of Raleigh was between Davie and South Streets. The land there was owned by James M. Harris, a white farmer and livery man. He and other real estate investors built tiny one-story homes and rented them out to Blacks. This area was composed of a mixture of Black and white blue-collar workers. Occupations of those in the southwest quadrant included work at the railroad yards, machine shops and gasworks.

The city commissioners complained about the moral climate of outlying Black districts after the war when there was a sharp rise in the Black population. The postwar white attitude was "racial claustrophobia." This term could be construed to mean several things:

1) Formerly enslaved people could and did roam the areas, particularly urban areas, at will. They were no longer under the control of slave masters and overseers. The loss of control over people who didn't look like them was frightening to many, probably most, whites.

2) Not only were formerly enslaved people whom urban dwellers had known moving freely throughout the city, but there was also a great influx of unknown formerly enslaved people in the area. Many of these people were from across the state.

The WPA slave narratives are full of interviews that detail people leaving plantations and farms when Union troops came through an area. They just followed the soldiers. They had nothing to take with them—no clothes, shoes, food, money, furniture. At this point, most former slaves had no idea what freedom was or what to do with it, and they were given little direction. They just knew that freedom was something they wanted and deserved as opposed to being completely and wholly under another person's control and being treated as objects.

3) Because of the costs of the Civil War, former plantation owners and slaveholders were also without funds or ready access to them. With the help of those former slaves still on their farms, they hid what goods and possessions they had, but if the Union soldiers found them, they usually confiscated them. (This doesn't excuse or explain anything but is just a fact. Very few gave any of what they had left to their former slaves.)

There was a feeling that Raleigh was under siege by displaced Black rural refugees, in fact by Blacks period. It was one thing for a large number of

Blacks who were under the complete control of the white population to be moving about the city. It was something completely bewildering for that population to have no control and in fact to be asked to share all of the things they had previously been in control of. So, ways had to be considered to bring that population back under the control of the white man.

Annexation brought segregated communities under the white authority of the city government so the police officers could oversee the activity in those Black communities. Generally, these were considered rough areas of town by the white elected officials. It was considered important to keep Negroes or Blacks out of the white neighborhoods because that prevented racial mixing and also prevented the lowering of property values. For Blacks, that wasn't a problem because it gave them access to jobs and welcome freedom from white surveillance, as well as allowing them to enjoy the company of other Blacks. However, this also caused limited housing options because of poverty and meant that Blacks lived in the worst parts of the city.

Whites preferred to live along the ridges and on top of hills. Therefore, they sold the low-lying ground near contaminated streams, horse slaughterhouses, flour mills, industrial sites and cemeteries because of the drainage and offensive odors that were in these places. Blacks were sold or offered land for lease or rented homes in places that were considered unfit for whites. Thus, the easiest way to locate Negro settlements in southern cities was to find the lowest spots in the area.

Many of the areas that Blacks lived in had extremely unsanitary conditions. They lived in alleys that were considered filthy, narrow places. These alleys had open sewers and were breeding grounds for disease. They were places where there was crime, and one source says that these were areas fit only for cattle. This is part of the reason for the high mortality rates among Black people.

These areas also lacked streetlights and running water, and there was rarely streetcar service. There was little, if any, fire protection in the area either. Black settlements were also placed in certain areas in order to restrict their political power. In Raleigh, Blacks were kept in the Second and Fourth Wards, preventing majorities in the other wards to keep Democratic control in place.

Deed covenants throughout the city of Raleigh's white subdivisions restricted ownership away from Black people regardless of economic ability. Acquiring housing in white neighborhoods that were bordering Black neighborhoods was called trickle-down housing and led to white flight from the areas, a trend that continued through the 1980s.

City Government.

Mayor—J. H. Separk.
Aldermen—*First Ward*—Jas. McKee, John Armstrong, H. J. Hamill. *Second Ward*—J. J. Nowell, W. H. Martin, Stewart Ellison. *Third Ward*—P. F. Pescud, Jr., John C. Blake, Wm. C. Stronach, R. H. Bradley, J. C. R. Little. *Fourth Ward*—H. C. Jones, James H. Jones, James H. Harris. *Fifth Ward*—P. C. Fleming, J. Ruffin Williams, R. H. Jones.
Treasurer—Leo. D. Heartt.
Clerk and Collector—George H. Williams.
Chief Police—B. C. Manly.

Top: Segregated public trolley system in Raleigh. *State Archives of North Carolina.*

Below: Election results for 1875, when Stewart Ellison (Second Ward) and all of the Fourth Ward aldermen were Black. *From* Daily Constitution, *July 5, 1875.*

Between 1860 and 1870, the Black population increased from 2,087 to 4,094, or 53 percent of the total population. The numbers could have been more because the federal census tended to undercount the number of Blacks. In 1860, 4,780 people lived in the city. Of these, 466 were free Blacks and lived scattered throughout the city. Some owned property within the original boundaries. An additional 1,621 were slaves who lived with their owners. That meant almost 44 percent of the population was Black.

The neighborhoods that were created after the war were created from the estate and plantation owners throughout the city. The names of the estates that were divided included Polk, Mordecai, Devereaux, O'Rorke,

Gatling, Barringer, Bledsoe, Manly, Cannon, Smith and Saunders. There were others around the city.

The freedmen settled in the areas east and south of the city. That would be east of East Street and south of South Street. Whites who owned one-half-acre or more lots subdivided their property. They sold small parcels to freedmen. This caused small Black enclaves among the white plantation owners. They were called salt and pepper areas. The southeastern and southwestern quadrants were divided and caused large Black majorities to live there. This just happened to be near the Raleigh and Gaston Railroad, where jobs were easier for those with little or no training to get, but eventually, the success of the train industry reversed and faltered, and people moved to the northwest, closer to other types of jobs. White people moved to the northeast and northwest quadrants.

Eastern lands were bounded by East Street, Market Street, John Gatling's land on the east, Watson's land to the south and the State Fairgrounds. The State Fairgrounds was at the corner of Tarboro Road and New Bern Avenue from 1853 to 1873. This was the main area where the freedmen settled because the fairgrounds was where the hospital had been during the war.

What had been considered fashionable white residential districts became residential centers for the growing Black populations. The concentration of freedmen at the fairgrounds provided the nucleus for freedmen's villages like St. Petersburg, Cotton Place, Idlewild, Old Fairgrounds and Hungry Neck. In the south, Hayti, Cannon Lands and Manly's Homestead were the freedmen's villages that were created. Another area where the freedmen settled was the Smith-Haywood Street area in East Raleigh. The south end of Wilmington Street and Blount Street adjoining the Moses Bledsoe property that was adjacent to Shaw University was another area. Outlying Black neighborhoods, away from the downtown area, allowed for lower property costs and more opportunity for home purchase. This would be seen in areas like Method, Oberlin, Nazareth and Lincolnville.

Black civic and religious institutions are important to note in terms of housing patterns and Black community growth. The number of Black schools, churches, businesses and other institutions depended on the Black community for survival and strength and fostered racial solidarity and segregation. In the mid-1880s, there were nine Black churches in Raleigh. Within ten years, South Raleigh's Black community below Davie Street had two graded schools and six additional churches, one of the two Black colleges, a Masonic Hall and the Institute for the Colored Deaf, Dumb and Blind.

BLACK CHURCH BEGINNINGS

Raleigh has a formidable history in terms of the Black church. The roots of the Black church go back to the times of slavery. Many plantation owners didn't want their slaves to know anything about religion. Others wanted slaves to hear those passages requiring slaves to obey their masters to keep fear and obedience hand-in-hand. Some slave owners, however, encouraged religious knowledge and brought it to their slaves and their slaves to the church. In some instances, plantation owners held services on Sunday mornings at home with a traveling preacher or small bits of Bible reading and prayer. Other owners ventured to church services and allowed slaves to worship and become members of an organized institution.

Many of Raleigh's oldest and largest churches began before slavery ended and had both Black and white members. In some instances, the enslaved Blacks' membership outnumbered the white parishioners. After slavery ended, Black members asked to start their own congregations and were granted permission to do so. The parent churches sometimes assisted in the process by purchasing and selling land or buildings or providing ministerial staff. There were six antebellum churches in the city. By 1871, there were fifteen churches—eleven white and four Black. The Methodist congregations were the only ones to form all-Black assemblies during the antebellum period. (Individual church histories will appear as part of the neighborhood discussions.)

HISTORY OF BLACK CHURCHES IN RALEIGH

Year Started	Original Church Name	Present Church Name
1812	First Baptist Church	First Baptist Church
1844–49	The African Church	St. Paul AME Church
1860s	Neville's Episcopal Church	no longer in existence
1863	Manly Street Christian Church	Macedonia Christian Church
1865	Second Baptist Church	Tupper Memorial Baptist Church
1865	Wilson Temple Church	Wilson Temple United Methodist Church
1867	St. Augustine's Protestant Episcopal Church	St. Ambrose Episcopal Church
1867	Little Methodists	St. Matthew AME
1868–72	Davie Street Presbyterian Church	Davie Street Presbyterian Church
1869	Martin Street Baptist Church	Martin Street Baptist Church
1872	Lincolnville AME Church	Lincolnville AME Church
1873	Oak City Baptist Church	Oak City Baptist Church
1878	First Baptist Church of Oberlin	Oberlin Baptist Church
1882	Rush Metropolitan Baptist Church	Rush Metropolitan Baptist Church
1886	St. James AME Church	St. James AME Church
1895	Fayetteville Street Baptist Church	First Cosmopolitan Baptist Church

General attitudes of whites toward Blacks did not get any better during this period. Settlements of free Blacks were described as "frail little huts occupied by barbers, fiddlers and jack-of-all-trades." There was a written complaint in 1865 from Mary B. Pettigrew to her brother that "Raleigh was offense with dirty negroes." A statement in the *Raleigh Weekly Progress* on September 26, 1867, commented on "the great mass of unbleached Americans overcrowding our beautiful city with a population that was being made a dangerous instrument in the hands of vicious men." Even though many white families considered their paternalistic attitudes toward Blacks to be a good thing, after slavery ended, there were angry families in Raleigh who had hard times controlling their house servants and talked privately of driving Blacks out of North Carolina during the summer of 1865. There was much racial strife in the city at that time. By 1896, most of Raleigh's white population was living in the northeast and northwest quadrants that were north of Hargett Street. These were segregated neighborhoods. The southern half of the city was Black.

BUSINESSES

W hile we tend to believe that East Hargett Street was Black Main Street in Raleigh, after slavery ended, it was mostly white businesses. By 1886, there were nineteen businesses on Wilmington Street, nine on Hargett Street and twenty other Black businesses in town.

The Black businesses were scattered along Fayetteville, Hargett and Wilmington Streets and Exchange Plaza in 1873. There were thirty-one Black businesses in the downtown area at that time, and they were run by people who worked with their hands—artisans and craftsmen. They included barbers, blacksmiths, butchers, carpenters, shoemakers, mechanics, tailors, textile workers and owners of restaurants, cafés and hotels. In a personal interview, it was revealed that between 1873 and 1874, a brick mason could earn three dollars a day. These wages helped this particular family move from Hungry Neck to Oberlin.

> *In 1875–76, for example, there were only six barbers in the entire community and all six were Negroes, two of the six barbering for Negroes and four for whites....In the same...period all "eating house" and huckster stalls were operated by Negroes, while the number of Negro blacksmiths exceeded the number of white blacksmiths....Variation in type of business operated by Negroes came with the advent of these: two Negro newspapers, an undertaker and two additional graded schools in 1880...one attorney and five saloon keepers in 1883; one bakery, two boarding houses, one*

contractor and builder, one upholsterer, one fish and five meat market operators in 1886; a billiard room, dyeing and cleaning establishment, and furniture dealer in 1887; a hotel, physician and surgeon in 1888; and the first Negro dentist in 1911–12.

Due to the lack of Jim Crow laws during Reconstruction, the most prominent businesses were first on Fayetteville Street and then on Wilmington Street, and the less prominent were on Hargett Street. By 1891,

the Raleigh community had among Negroes, 17 brick masons, 34 carpenters, 32 draymen, 19 mechanics, 4 painters, 8 plasterers and whitewashers, 6 printers, 16 shoemakers, and 2 tinners. The professional field broadened also with more lawyers, physicians, ministers, nurses, and teachers. The co-existence, however, of 275 "colored" washerwomen, 361 servants, 42 seamstresses, 113 porters, and 349 laborers—all listed in the 1891 City Directory—must not be overlooked as suggestive of the chief occupations of the Negro.

There was dominance for Black entrepreneurs in certain trades. In 1891, twenty of twenty-two barbers were Black. All barbers for white customers were on Fayetteville Street with the exception of the Otey shop, situated in the Yarborough Hotel. Willie Otey Kay, the highly skilled dressmaker, stated in an interview that part of the reason she was able to dress so many white women was because her father passed along her name in his barbershop to prominent white men.

There was a monopoly of eating houses or restaurants owned by Blacks at this time also. Whites could eat in "colored" places, although "coloreds"

Postcard advertisement for Busy Bee Café on South Wilmington Street that eventually moved to the Lightner Arcade on Hargett Street. *State Archives of North Carolina.*

RALEIGH RETAIL PRICES.

ARTICLES.	PRICES.	
COUNTRY PRODUCE.		
APPLES Green,	1 25 @	2 00
" Dried,	0 08 @	10
BUTTER Best country,	0 30 @	35
" Good "	0 25 @	30
" Goshen,	0 45 @	50
BACON—N. C. Sides,	0 00 @	14
" Hams,	0 00 @	17½
" " Sh'uldrs,	0 00 @	12½
CHICKENS—	25. 30 @	35
DUCKS—	0 00 @	35
EGGS—	0 15 @	17¼
FLOUR- N. C. Family,	0 00 @	9 50
" Extra,	0 00 @	9 00
FODDER—Per 100 lbs.,	0 00 @	2 00
HAY—Per 100 lbs.,	1 15 @	1 25
CORN—	1 00 @	1 00
MEAL—	0 00 @	1 00
POTATOES—Sweet,	0 75 @	85
" N. C. Irish,	0 75 @	1 00
OATS—Bailed ⅌ 100 lbs.,	0 00 @	1 50
" Seed ⅌ bushel,	0 00 @	80
	@	00
	@	00
	@	00
GROCERIES.		
BACON—Rib Bulk Side,	0 00 @	10
" C. R. "	0 00 @	10½
" " Smok'd "	0 00 @	11
" Shoulders,	0 00 @	9½
" Best Sugar-cured Hams,	0 00 @	14½
COFFEE—Old gov'ment,	0 00 @	40
" Laguira,	0 00 @	37¼
" Rio Prime,	0 00 @	36
" Good,	0 00 @	32¼
FISH—Mackerel, No. 3,	0 00 @	13 50
" N. C. Her'ngs,cut	0 00 @	8 25
" " Roe "	0 00 @	12 00
" Corn Shad, ½ bbl	0 00 @	10 00
FLOUR—Patapsco,	0 00 @	13 00
" Va. Family,	0 00 @	12 50
" Extra,	8 50 @	10 00
" Superfine,	6 50 @	8 00
MOLASSES—Cuba, new crop, ⅌ bbl	0 00 @	50
" " hhd	0 00 @	45
RICE—	0 00 @	10
SUGAR—Stand'd A ⅌ bbl	0 00 @	12½
" Extra C,	0 00 @	12
" Yellow,	0 10 @	11
SYRUP—Bbl.,	0 00 @	32¼

Advertisement showing Raleigh retail food prices. *From the* Weekly Era, *February 26, 1874.*

couldn't eat in their facilities. Many white people would patronize these eating establishments because they liked a particular "Mammy's" cooking. Other businesses where there was a dominance for Black entrepreneurs were in boardinghouses and meat and fish markets. Skilled trades where Blacks were dominant included shoemaking, blacksmithing and upholstery.

When Black businesses are discussed after Reconstruction and in the early part of the 1900s, people tend to think of Hargett Street, which was considered Black Main Street. While this information is generally correct, we also need to look at the City Market and neighborhood businesses.

City Market was originally located on Wilmington Street, where Exchange Plaza is today. At one point, the land was owned by Berry O'Kelly. There was cattle in the back of the market. The City of Raleigh owned the marketplace. The Board of Health wanted the city to fix the unsanitary conditions, and they did not. In 1914, the market was built in its present location.

Vendors at the market sold to anyone who came in and shopped. Regular vendors had spaces or stalls on the inside of the building. Tables that were set up outside the building were available for daily or weekly rent. On Friday and Saturday, farmers from out of town would pull in, park and sell from their horses, trucks, carriages or buggies across the street from the market.

The City Market was open six days a week. On Wednesdays, it closed at 6:00 p.m. On Saturdays, it closed at 10:00 p.m. In an interview for the book *Culture Town*, Rufus Hodge stated that people would come to town and visit. Moore Square had groves of trees, and people would spread blankets and eat from their baskets and make their own fun. The water fountains had step-on pedals instead of electric pumps. The water would splash up in the air. In the early 1930s, there were different types of entertainment on Moore

Hamlin Drug Store, originally People Drug Store, on Hargett Street (Black Main Street). This was the first Black licensed drugstore in the state, circa 1905. *State Archives of North Carolina.*

Square. Sometimes old man Moe Watson and his String Band would play. There were groups of Black men playing violin or guitar, and there were washboard bands. Hodge said that there was a family feel to the area. All parents looked out for one another's children regardless of race and looked out for one another's needs.

As whites started to patronize more white businesses as Jim Crow laws increased, Black Main Street did move to Hargett Street. Between 1900 and 1920, the number of Black-owned businesses on Hargett Street grew from nine to fifty. Other than white people patronizing their own businesses, Black businesses were pushed there because whites stopped leasing property to them in other areas. Black businesses tended to be around Moore Square because that was the commercial line between the Blacks and the whites.

Businesses

Last Name	First Name	Name of Business	Type of Business	Fourth Ward	Downtown	Oberlin	Third Ward	Notes
Taylor	Ransom	Dewey Leake's Funeral Home	funeral home	X				
Burwell	Mrs. L.S.		trash pickup, clean outside bathrooms	X				
			store	corner Manly and Worth				
		Prather's Store		Cannon Street				
Arnold	Hugh			Cannon and Canister				
		White Rose Grocery Store	grocery store	Harrington and South				
		Moe Ziegler Store	grocery store	West and South				Run by Greeks and Jews
Mosley	Mrs. Patti		caterer	X				
Evans	Mr.		gas station	South and McDowell				
		Fourth Ward Pressing Club		Plummer and Vine				

Last Name	First Name	Name of Business	Type of Business	Fourth Ward	Downtown	Oberlin	Third Ward	Notes
McNeill	Mr.		retread tires/ vulcanizing business	X				learned how to box there
Castleberry	Fred	Castleberry's Shop	shoe shop	X				
Rice	Sam and Alice		confectionary shop	X				had two stores, one by high school; brought goods to Washington before they had a cafeteria
Jackson	Willie		shoeshine shop	McDowell Street				
Humphrey			barber	McDowell				
Joyner		Jones Beauty Shop	beauty shop	McDowell				
Massenburg	Kenny		café	South Street				
Jeffers	J.		snowball stand	South Street				
		Mitchell's Tire Shop		X				

Last Name	First Name	Name of Business	Type of Business	Fourth Ward	Downtown	Oberlin	Third Ward	Notes
		Marrow Store		Fayetteville Street				
McClain	Jim		wood yard	X				
Yeargan	J.W.		iron foundry	Fayetteville Street				
Williams	Bob	Bob Williams Drug Store	coke, ice cream cones	McDowell, Dawson and Cabarrus				
		Pine Drug Store		S. Saunders Street				white owned
Hoffman	Kenny			X				had cows at his house, plowed gardens for people
Minters			cleaners	X				
Ligon	J.W.	*Union Reformer*	newspaper, corner store		1917 office on Wilmington; 1920 office on Hargett		X	

Last Name	First Name	Name of Business	Type of Business	Fourth Ward	Downtown	Oberlin	Third Ward	Notes
Harris	Samuel C.	Harris Barber College	barbershop and barber college		Wilmington Street then Hargett Street then Blount Street		X	
Delany	Dr. Lemuel		physician		Hoover Building on Hargett			1923
Roberts	Dr.		physician		Hoover Building on Hargett			1923
Edwards	Dr.		physician		Hoover Building on Hargett			1923
Hall	P.T.		restaurant		Wilmington Street and Lightner Arcade on Hargett			1921
Constance	Frank		pool room		Wilmington to Lightner Arcade to Hargett to Arcade			partnership split; business destroyed by Lightner Arcade fire

Last Name	First Name	Name of Business	Type of Business	Fourth Ward	Downtown	Oberlin	Third Ward	Notes
Taylor	Jimmy		pool room		Wilmington to Lightner Arcade to Hargett to Arcade			partnership split; business destroyed by Lightner Arcade fire
		Bee Hive Café	restaurant		Hargett Street Lightner Arcade			
Frasier	Mac		clothing store		Hargett Street			haberdashery where Turner's used to be
Silver			shoe store		X			
Lightner	Calvin	Lightner Arcade, Lightner Funeral Home	hotel; restaurant; other businesses; apartments; undertaker; contractor		X			
Young, then Hamlin		Hamlin Drug	pharmacy		X			People's Drug, then Hamlin Drug
		Mallette's Drug Store	pharmacy		X			

Last Name	First Name	Name of Business	Type of Business	Fourth Ward	Downtown	Oberlin	Third Ward	Notes
Hamlin	Tom	Community Drug Store	pharmacy		Hargett then Blount			sold to William P. Wimberley
Wimberley	Richard E.	Central Drug Store	pharmacy					corner Swain and Davie
		NC Teacher Association	Black teachers' group		Hargett			
Edmunds	Mrs.		dress shop		X			Mrs. Roberts was next owner
			doctor/dentist offices		corner Hargett and Wilmington			
Wilson			barbershop		X			
Lee	Mollie Huston	Richard B. Harrison Library	library		Hargett in Delany Building then S. Blount Street			
Evans	Dr. George		dentist		Delany Building			after 1938

Last Name	First Name	Name of Business	Type of Business	Fourth Ward	Downtown	Oberlin	Third Ward	Notes
Lewis	Mr. Needham and Mrs. Hattie J. Wooten	Lewis Hotel	hotel; boardinghouse				220 East Cabarrus Street	two buildings with 26 rooms; had cafeteria and shoeshine parlor in one building; second building was two-story hotel, 1948, at death of Mrs. Lewis, changed to Deluxe Hotel
Lane	Major George L.		mortuary, coffin and furniture maker, meat market owner		X			
			pool room		X			
			cab stand		X			
		Lassiter's Hardware	hardware store		X			
		Hayes-Jackson appliance	appliance store		X			

Last Name	First Name	Name of Business	Type of Business	Fourth Ward	Downtown	Oberlin	Third Ward	Notes
Hoover		Hoover's Dry Goods Store	general store		Wilmington Street between Hargett and Martin			
Roberts	Mrs.		millinery store		X			
			bars		X			
Capehart	Dr. L.B.		physician		Wilmington Street			
Dunston	Dr.		physician		Wilmington Street			
		Prince Hall Masonic Temple					Cabarrus and Blount	
Scott	Jim		meat/butcher shop		City Market			
Crenshaw			meat/butcher shop		City Market			
Thigpen	Zeb		meat/butcher shop		City Market			

Last Name	First Name	Name of Business	Type of Business	Fourth Ward	Downtown	Oberlin	Third Ward	Notes
Chamblee	Abe		meat/butcher shop		City Market			
Hodge	Ed		meat/butcher shop		City Market			
Hodge	Robert		fish market		City Market			
Rochelle	John		fish market		City Market			
Grant	Will		general store			X		
Thornton	James		drugstore			X		
Ellerbe			barbershop			X		
Hall	Plummer and Della		general store			X		
Shepherd	Baholm		general stores (two)			X		
Smith	Louis		shoe shop			X		
Latta	Reverend M.L.		general store			X		
Morgan	Rose		general store			X		
Hite	Mumford		general store			X		
			pressing club			X		

Last Name	First Name	Name of Business	Type of Business	Fourth Ward	Downtown	Oberlin	Third Ward	Notes
Graves	Willis		post office/store			X		
			miniature golf course			X		
Turner	John		shoe store		X			
Haywood	Claude		blacksmith			X		
Hunter	Robert		carpet maker			X		
Thomas	Dave		drayman			X		
Haywood	Charles A.	Raleigh Funeral Home	undertaker				X	
Love	James	Esso	gas station				X	
Anderson	Virgil		shoe shop				X	
Burns	Tony		restaurant				X	
Hodge	Reuben		farmer				X	
Lane	Allen		stonecutter				X	
Marshall	Henry		stonecutter				X	
Matthews	William		stonecutter					
Williams	Dr. Peter		physician				X	

Last Name	First Name	Name of Business	Type of Business	Fourth Ward	Downtown	Oberlin	Third Ward	Notes
Frazier	Charles	Capital Building and Loan Assn.					X	
Edwards	Gaston		architect					
Pope	Dr. Manassa		physician				X	
Evans	Henry and John		carpenters				X	
Williams	Charles		attorney				X	
Cumbo	Frank		barber				X	
Dunston	Royal		plasterer				X	
Roberts	Samuel		bricklayer				X	
Noble	Ferry		barber				X	
Hayes	Thomas		plasterer				X	
Jones	Hurley		bricklayer				X	

Between 1891 and 1917, Shaw University's Leonard School of Medicine and Pharmacy, as well as its Law School, graduated students who planted roots after completing their studies. The city directories show that between 1900 and 1920, there were increases in some Black businesses. Black lawyers increased from two to thirteen, and tailors increased from one to five. Other businesses that saw increases included contractors, druggists, grocers, insurance agents, eating houses, shoe dealers and cleaners.

By 1921, Jim Crow laws had rapidly been put on the law books and white owners stopped renting space to Black business owners. Many Black businessmen had purchased property on Hargett Street and so remained there. Between the population growth and Jim Crow laws, small businesses in the neighborhoods increased. Grocery stores began to show up on street corners in the mid-1920s. There were fifty Black-owned markets in the city, and only two of those were downtown on Hargett Street. By 1928, barbershops had moved into neighborhoods as well. Nine out of thirteen were outside the business district.

Several land companies started during Reconstruction to assist freedmen in making purchases of land and building homes. They were:

- Raleigh Cooperative Land and Building Association
- National Freedmen's Savings and Trust Company
- Union Enterprise Company
- North Carolina Land Company
- Raleigh Land and Improvement Company

The Raleigh Cooperative Land and Building Association was founded by James H. Harris, the president. S.S. Ashley, a minister, was the secretary. J. Brinton Smith, principal of St. Augustine's Normal School, was the treasurer. This was the first mortgage cooperative in the state of North Carolina and operated for ten years. It loaned money to freedmen for land purchases and building loans. Loans were payable back to the organization at ten dollars a month. The loans were primarily in areas such as Oberlin Village, Cotton Place and Hungry Neck. It was also a real estate firm. It was the principal developer of Idlewild, as well as St. Petersburg and Hungry Neck.

An example of the association's business initiative is regarding Amos Brooks and his wife, Anna Eliza Ligon. They were not slaves. He worked for Baker's Livery Stables, and she was a washerwoman. On July 15, 1869, Amos became a member of the association and purchased two shares. This allowed him to buy property that cost $400.

The North Carolina Land Company was established in 1869. George Little was the president. The other officers included George W. Swepson,

James Love, owner of Esso (forerunner of Exxon) gas station in Raleigh. *State Archives of North Carolina.*

R.W. Best and Richard Kingsland. They published a 136-page book that extolled "investment opportunities in the state." Their book talked about Wake County's productive and cheap land. This group purchased land in Cotton Place and Oberlin. Freedmen were the principal purchasers from the North Carolina Land Company. In 1871, the General Assembly passed

Above, left: Tucker Hall, site of the North Carolina Land Company office on Fayetteville Street, established in 1869. *The Albert Barden Collection, State Archives of North Carolina.*

Above, right: The Raleigh branch of Mechanics and Farmers Bank opened in 1923 on Hargett Street (chartered in 1907 in Durham). It didn't fail after the 1929 stock crash. *The Albert Barden Collection, State Archives of North Carolina.*

Left: Description of Idlewild property for sale and increase in Raleigh property values forecasted for future. *From the* Evening Visitor, *June 15, 1891.*

"Idlewild."

This beautiful suburban property is being rapidly closed out at the reasonable rates fixed in the printed schedule of the Raleigh Land and Improvement Company. About half of the property has already been sold to our very best citizens, many of whom intend to build at once. This has been accomplished without fuss or parade, or any questionable method. The property has sold itself. We desire to say to those in or out of the city who may wish to make a safe and buying investment, that if they will let us know, we will ta e pleasure in showing them the prop٤ erty, and will call at the train or residence for that purpose. Those in the State living upon railroads and who come to the city and purchasing any of this property through us will have their railroad fair refunded by us.

It is the opinion of the best judges of such matters that real estate in and around Raleigh will very rapidly increase in value in the near future. The electric railway now being built insures this in regard to property so favorably situated as "Idlewild."

With the electric railway now in process of construction and the industries being started in and around Raleigh the population of the city must largely increase and hence real estate will increase rapidly in value, especially real estate situated in the new town, "Idlewild."

Those desiring information in regard to this property will do well to let us know.

J. M. BROUGHTON & Co.,
je13 2t.   Agents.

a resolution naming Little as commissioner of immigration for the state of North Carolina.

Raleigh Land and Improvement Company purchased land from Cotton's Plantation. It called the development Idlewild. In 1891, it laid out one hundred lots on the hill overlooking Hungry Neck. The lots located near New Bern Avenue were purchased by white people. In 1893, sixty-four additional lots were plotted to Tarboro Road. This area was going to also be developed as a white neighborhood. However, the lots between New Bern and Oakwood did not sell as quickly as anticipated. The lots on the higher ground were more desirable land. Eventually, those lots were lost at public auction. After the war, many plantations had to be sold for taxes that were not able to be paid because of the war. In 1869, twenty-three Wake County plantations containing almost eight thousand acres of land were sold for taxes and brought in $7,718.

The National Freedmen's Savings and Trust Company was also started in the area. This was not a direct program of the Freedmen's Bureau. The officers and directors were Governor William Holden, George Swepson, R.W. Pulliam, J.T. Deweese and James H. Harris. This organization was chartered by Congress to aid Blacks financially. The Wake County branch was located at the corner of Fayetteville and Hargett Streets. The cashier was G.W. Brody. Deposits were accepted at this financial institution from five cents upward. In 1871, the Savings and Trust showed healthy growth. In 1874, the national institution failed, and thus, so did the local ones.

FREEDMEN'S BUREAU

The U.S. Bureau of Refugees, Freedmen and Abandoned Lands (Freedmen's Bureau) was established by the federal government in the War Department on March 3, 1865. The responsibilities of the bureau were to assist former slaves and impoverished whites, as well as those who had become destitute because of the Civil War, in:
- "finding employment";
- "establishing schools";
- "buying or renting land" (including trying to settle former slaves on abandoned or confiscated land);
- "combating disease and poverty because of displacement"; and
- "assisting with food and clothing."

This also included operating hospitals and temporary camps, locating family members, helping freedmen to legalize marriages, supervising labor contracts, providing legal representation, investigating racial confrontations and working with Black soldiers, sailors and their heirs to get back pay, bounty payments and pensions.

The North Carolina commissioner of the Freedmen's Bureau was General Oliver Otis Howard. He had several lieutenants with him. U.S. Army Private Samuel Riddick was a runaway slave who worked directly under him. Private Riddick was from Perquimans County and had been captured during the war in Virginia. He learned to read and write in a Freedmen's Bureau school, and once he came to Raleigh, he remained here the rest of his life. The bureau operated for three and a half years before it was shut down.

Postcard of Peace College (William Peace University), originally home to the offices of the Freedmen's Bureau during Reconstruction. *Durwood Barbour Collection of North Carolina Postcards, State Archives of North Carolina.*

Food rations that were given to those in need included hardtack or crackers, pickled or saltpeter meat and occasionally white potatoes or molasses. The supply branch of the Freedmen's Bureau was closed in the summer of 1869, and the troops were removed in 1870. The Educational Department was under the leadership of Dr. H.C. Vogel. The establishment of schools in the area was considered far-reaching. The bureau also dispensed medical aid and assisted former slaves in labor contracts with white employers or former slave masters.

EDUCATION AND RALEIGH'S BLACK SCHOOLS

On November 15, 1830, the North Carolina Constitution was amended to deny the right of education to Blacks and slaves. After the emancipation of the slaves, the Freedmen's Bureau and other agencies (usually northern missionary societies) created schools throughout the South in order to teach formerly enslaved people how to read and write. Blacks recognized their need for help with education. The freedmen's desire to learn encouraged the white missionaries who came from the North.

Prior to the establishment of the white Centennial Graded School in 1876, public schools in Raleigh were taught in small houses throughout the township. There was no supervision for these schools except by the local school committee. The committee put all the funds for education into one pot and established one school for the white children. This was the second graded school in the state.

As northern missionaries came into Raleigh to help teach, they had a hard time finding lodging in the white community. They tended to find lodging with mulattos because those families needed income. Sometimes, hotel dining rooms were used to teach Black students in Raleigh. At some point, it was announced that no Black man, woman or child could attend school and remain in the jobs that they had. In fact, some white people said that a sudden increase in sickness was because the northern people had arrived to teach and brought sickness with them.

In 1877, the township school committee had three members: Chairman Colonel A.W. Schaffer, Secretary M.V. Gilbert and H.C. Jones (colored).

Teacher's *First* Grade Certificate.

The Examiner certifies that he has thoroughly and fully examined *Chas. N. Hunter*, an applicant for a Teacher's Certificate, on the several branches of study named below, and that *his* true grade of scholarship in each is indicated by the figure annexed to it: figure 1 indicating the highest, and figure 5 the lowest grade:

Reading,	1
Writing,	2
Sounds of Marked Letters,	2
Spelling and Rules of Spelling,	1
Mental Arithmetic,	1
Written Arithmetic,	1
English Grammar and Analysis,	1
Composition and Rhetoric,	
Geography and Map Drawing,	1
History,	
Drawing,	
Making and Keeping School Register,	1

The said applicant has also furnished satisfactory evidence of good moral character. This certificate will therefore authorize the said *Chas. N. Hunter* to teach in the Public Schools in *Wake* County one year from the date hereof. This *16* day of *Mar*, 187*8* :

Jno. E. Dugger
Examiner.

The 1878 teacher certificate of Charles N. Hunter. It is rated by the teacher's accomplishment, not the grade level of Wake County students. This was the highest grade of certificate. *Charles N. Hunter Scrapbook, Duke University Papers.*

Captain John Duggar of Warrenton, North Carolina, a Confederate war veteran, was principal of the school. In 1880, there were buildings for two colored schools: Washington Graded School and Garfield School. The East Raleigh schools were in the Old Fairgrounds neighborhood. They were not church-related.

The 1883 Raleigh Township School Board was made up of Needham B. Broughton, S.W. Whiting and C.B. Root. Under the administration of Andrew J. McAlpine, from Buncombe County, there was one white school, Centennial Graded, and four colored schools: Johnson (which closed in 1884), Washington, Garfield and Oberlin.

Under McAlpine, the salaries were as follows: white principals made $1,200 a year; colored principals made $50 a month; male teachers made $50 a month; and female teachers made $40 a month. In 1885, both Washington and Garfield Schools were enlarged and improved. Members of the school board committee at that time were W.S. Primrose, Mills Brown and Needham B. Broughton.

From 1885 to 1895, the schools were under the administration of Edward P. Moses. The Raleigh school committee in 1885 consisted of Reverend F.L. Reed, G. Rosenthal, R.H. Lewis, T.H. Briggs Jr., S.F. Mordecai and Needham B. Broughton. From 1888 to 1899, there was mention made of creating a high school for Negroes, but it was met with opposition. All schools were closed after five months, after struggling to raise funds. No bond was issued to help pay for them.

On March 16, 1889, a school census was taken. There were 4,548 persons enrolled in school from ages six through twenty-one. There were 1,113 white students and 1,401 colored students. During this time, there was one white school, the Centennial Graded School, and three colored schools: Washington, Garfield and Oberlin.

Information about the Raleigh Public School administration of Frank Harper. *From* Barbee Historical Sketch of Raleigh Public Schools, *Mrs. J.H. Barbee.*

Under the administration of Superintendent Logan D. Howell, from 1895 to 1898, Crosby School was opened. A new Garfield School was erected near Crosby School. There was a requirement that all teachers now be trained. For the first time in sixteen years, there was a seat for every student, white and colored.

In 1903, there were forty-nine white teachers with combined salaries of $12,075.72 and thirty-four colored teachers with combined salaries of $7,049.50. In 1904–05, a compulsory school law was enacted for Raleigh Township.

In 1917, the Black citizens petitioned for high school funding in the city. Up until this time, the city had agreed to pay tuition at Shaw and St. Augustine's for those who wanted to attend high school. (Mildred James was in the first group of students who attended St. Augustine's Normal School under the arrangement where the city paid $1.50 a month for Black students to attend high school.) A group of Black women called the Colored Women's Association went to the commissioner and the superintendent to request the high school, and it was finally approved.

The Johnson School

The Johnson School was organized in 1865 by the friends of the Freedmen's Aid Society of Pennsylvania. Anne Fannie Graves was the principal of the school. There were more than three hundred students in attendance. The building the school met in was on St. Paul AME Church's lot at the corner of West and Edenton Streets in 1867. By 1869, there were five teachers who conducted classes at four different levels. The levels were primary, intermediate, advanced and normal.

Former slaves reminisced about the school. Barbara Haywood said that her family moved to Davie Street from the John Walton Plantation, and this was where she attended school. Charlie H. Hunter stated that he learned to read and write in the school taught by the northern folk after the surrender. "Mister and Missus Graves taught in Raleigh at the rear of the AME Church."

THE EPISCOPAL PARISH SCHOOL

The school was established by local Black leaders. It was organized in 1866 as the Colored Educational Association of North Carolina and chartered by the General Assembly in 1867. The names on the list of incorporators include James H. Harris, Moses Patterson, Hardy Lockhart, W.H. Anderson, John P. Caswell, W.H. Matthews, Robert White, Wilson Morgan and J.E. O'Hara.

The work was delayed on the school. Harris and Patterson, joined by Alex Long, Benjamin Rhodes and Oliver Rhone, formed a separate board of trustees under the newly organized Negro Episcopal Church that had been St. Augustine's and later became St. Ambrose. They received permission from the General Assembly to use a lot at the corner of Lane and Dawson Streets for "Education of children residing in and near the City of Raleigh." A sum of $5,000 was appropriated for use by the Freedmen's Bureau. The building was completed and occupied. The parish school and the church had some difficulties. The school foundered and was reopened in 1895.

LINCOLN DAY SCHOOL

This school was organized in 1865 in the old Guion Hotel. It was started by a missionary named Leland from the New England Freedmen's Commission and the Lincoln Sunday School. Teachers assisted from the Friends Freedmen's Aid Society for a year. The school was closed at the end of 1868.

THE MILES SCHOOL

The school was named in honor of Union General Nelson A. Miles, who was in charge of the local Freedmen's Bureau. The school was opened on May 25, 1868. The first teacher was J.E. O'Hara. The building the school was housed in sat on North Salisbury Street between North and Johnson Streets. It was built by the Freedmen's Bureau. Black members of First Baptist Church bought the lot and continued the school there for a number of years. The first pastor of First Baptist Church, Reverend W.M. Warwick, and his sister Louisa Warrick were the teachers. Students became part of the Raleigh Public Schools in the 1870s.

GARFIELD SCHOOL

In 1878, the school that became Crosby-Garfield was first named the East Raleigh School. In 1881, the name was changed to Garfield School. W.L. Crosby was the principal. The school was organized in a small church building on East Davie Street. Charles N. Hunter was in charge of the school. It moved to Swain Street into a building once used by Second Baptist Church. Land was purchased by the school board in 1889. In 1897,

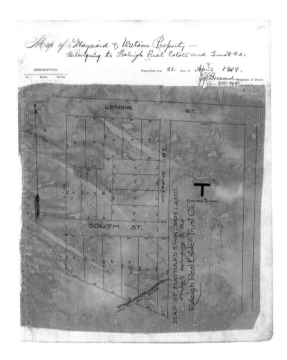

Above: A land transfer map from Watson to Raleigh Real Estate and Trust Company (Lenoir and South Streets). Watson mansion became Garfield School, located at the T. *Wake County Register of Deeds.*

Right: An article on Garfield School exercises written by Charles N. Hunter, school headmaster, in the *Raleigh Evening Visitor*, November 7, 1894. *Charles N. Hunter Scrapbook, Duke University Papers.*

RALEIGH'S SCHOOLS.

The Garfield Colored School Excellently Conducted.

The Garfield school, the smaller of the two city public schools for colored children, is a splendidly conducted institution.

A VISITOR reporter called there this morning and was struck with the discipline and order that prevailed and with the general excellence of the school work. The school needs another building badly, although an addition has already been made.

As at the Washington school, colored children, both male and female, are admitted and there are now 325 children enrolled. This number will be greatly increased during the spring term. The ages of the students run from 5 to 17 years. Besides the principal, C. N. Hunter, and his assistant, Mrs. A. P. Martin, there are three teachers, Miss Nichols, Miss Love and Miss McGary. There are now four recitation rooms, two of which open on the assembly room in which the farthest advanced students sit. The other two rooms are given up to the primary department which is so large that the day is divided, half coming to school in the morning and half in the afternoon. In this department as in the primary department at the white schools, the little students are taught to read and spell by the sound method.

The reporter saw a class of beginners, about 5 and 6 years old, recite and it is wonderful how the little ones make progress. They did fully as well as the white children and considering the advantages they have had, their recitation was truly wonderful.

The same "system" that was started by Prof. Moses and that has placed Raleigh's public schools on such a high plane, is in vogue here. The students at the Garfield after having advanced as far as the 5th grade, according to the old system, are transferred to the larger Washington school.

the Watson estate was purchased by the school board to be used for the school. After repairs to the original building, it was used to relieve crowded conditions at Garfield School.

A Negro educator connected with Shaw University, Henry Crosby, left money in his estate for repairs and to purchase a new building. In 1910, the Chavis and Garfield Schools were sold, and Garfield School moved to the property on South Lenoir Street where the building presently stands. The new Garfield School was a two-story brick school with eight rooms, and John W. Ligon was the principal. Julia A. Williams was the principal of Crosby School. In 1920, the two schools were consolidated as Crosby-Garfield. Crosby was a primary school, and Garfield was the grammar or secondary school.

In 1935, the Garfield section of the school was damaged by fire. Students attended Lucille Hunter School until the repairs were made. The Crosby section of the school was torn down. In 1939, a modern school was built. At that time, the enrollment was 736 students in grades one through seven. There were 19 teachers in twenty classrooms. There were 722 books in the library, and PTA membership numbered one hundred.

THE CHAVIS SCHOOL

The Chavis School was begun in 1903. It was situated on the Harvey property at 508 South West Street and cost $3,000 to purchase. This was a high school and industrial school for Negro students. A colored teacher from Washington, D.C., was employed in the industrial section and complained about the lack of equipment for teaching students. One of the principals of the school was J.W. Paisley. He taught eighth and ninth grades. Louise Jeffries taught seventh grade. There were small classes. The school was closed between 1907 and 1908. The property was sold in 1910 along with the Garfield School.

LUCILLE HUNTER SCHOOL

The address of the school is 1018 East Davie Street. It was built in 1927. It was brick, fireproof and modern. The name was requested by Lucille

The stone quarry marker refers to an area near Lucille Hunter School (built circa 1920s). Granite from the quarry was used to construct the state capitol. *City of Raleigh.*

Hunter's former students. There were twenty classrooms, an auditorium, a library, a cafeteria and a clinic room. The school housed grades one through seven. There was a rock quarry close to the school that was closed and covered with grass.

WASHINGTON GRADED SCHOOL

Washington Graded School was a freedmen's school. Reverend Fisk P. Brewer of the American Missionary Association of New York started the school out of the church, First Congregational Church, which began in 1866. Classes were taught in the old chapel of the church. The first principal, after Reverend Brewer, was Esther P. Hayes. The one-room school became First Congregational Church and was situated at the corner of South and Manly Streets.

Reverend Brewer purchased a six-acre tract near the old Governor's Palace on South Street that was between McDowell and Manly Streets, and the school was built there. According to an interview for the book *Culture Town*, Louis Dunbar stated that it was a rambling green wooden frame building. It was also described as a fire trap with no conveniences. This school was only used for elementary grades. Reverend Brewer divided part of that property into small inexpensive lots and sold it to freedmen for their homes.

Before the school was completed in 1867, Brewer and his sister Adele Brewer taught classes in a rented building on Hargett Street. As of December 1866, fifteen of the fifty-seven students were white. "They attended school when they didn't have to work picking cotton." As of February 1867, all white children had left the school. They preferred no schooling as opposed to being ridiculed for attending school with Black students. In the second year of the school, there were seventy pupils during the day, and Hayes had twenty-five adults in school at night.

In December 1867, the school moved into a two-story wooden building that had been designed by Reverend Brewer and funded by the Freedmen's Bureau. The school had partially been built by parents of the pupils. The enrollment doubled, and many of the adults had to be turned away from night school. There were thirty-four desks accommodating three pupils each, along with two stoves, blackboards and maps.

By 1869, a second smaller building had been completed. They were able to continue classes as well as host a Sunday school. They rented a larger building to the state for a Negro school for the deaf and blind. It remained an American Missionary Association school until 1877, when the Raleigh Township school system began. After realizing that music was fundamental to the education of the students, the Congregational missionary teachers succeeded in getting northern sponsors to send a cabinet organ for both vocal instruction and religious services.

In 1885, the school was enlarged and improved upon. Principals of the school included Attorney E.A. Johnson in 1885; Reverend Alfred Davis, a Presbyterian minister; Dr. Lovelace B. Capehart; Professor John Branch; and, in 1916, Professor J.L. Levister.

Land was purchased for the new Washington School by the school board in 1889. By 1916, the desire in the community for a Black high school had increased. By this time, there was a public high school for white students. Shaw University and St. Augustine's College both discontinued their high school departments after 1921. Elementary students had nowhere to go for advanced work.

Superintendent S.M. Underwood and Mayor Culbreth, who was chair of the Raleigh School Board, asked the "colored men" to assist in site selection

The 1869 Washington Graded School Building (green wooden frame building on Lenoir Street) housed students in grades one through seven. *The Albert Barden Collection, State Archives of North Carolina.*

for a new high school. There was opposition to the site that was selected. Once this school was established on Fayetteville Street, it became a major reason for the exodus of white people from that area. Well into the twentieth century, the neighborhood with rental housing was 100 percent Black. The site was selected because it was considered a central location for Black students. It was the only Negro public school in the country located on the main street in the capital of any state.

Professor Levister was the first principal of the combined elementary and high school. He served two years in this role. When the two schools were divided, Professor Levister went to the elementary school. Mr. L.S. Cozart served as principal for two years following that, and the first graduating class was in 1927. Mr. M.W. Aiken followed as principal of the high school. Then there was a combined principal for twenty years.

Mr. J.W. Yeargin remembers fondly that there was a beautiful hillside for the school with very few trees, shrubs or wildflowers. He said there was an old mill house called Holman's Mill at the lower end of the property with

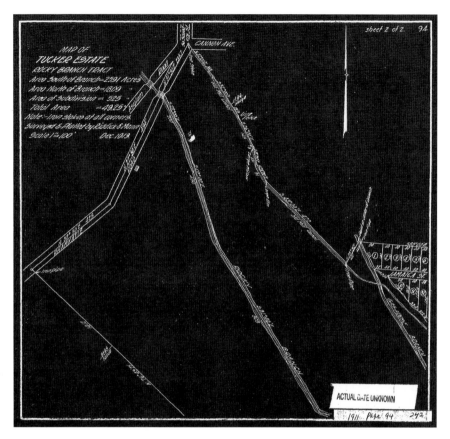

Rocky Branch Tract of Tucker Estates, showing Mount Hope Cemetery (Negro) on Fayetteville Street and Hayti Community. Washington School was built in between these two areas. *Wake County Register of Deeds.*

a stone dam that crossed Rocky Branch. The millpond covered the athletic field. At the completion of the building phase, there was no money left in the budget for landscaping. The school board asked the landscape gardeners at North Carolina State University what to do and were advised to plant trees and shrubbery on the hillside. Yeargin, president of the school's first PTA, stated that he "had some influence with the Public Works Administration." He was able to get laborers, more than one hundred men, "at seventy-five cents or a dollar a day, to move land and to create terraces in front of the school." The PTA raised money for cement, and he donated gravel and sand from a gravel pit and foundry that he owned on South Saunders Street.

The idea for a statewide PTA came from the Washington PTA under the leadership of Anna W. Holland. Raleigh was made the permanent meeting

Washington School (1923) replaced the original school, which burned. The high school had a wing added for the elementary school. It presently serves as an elementary school. *The Albert Barden Collection, State Archives of North Carolina.*

place. In 1927, fourteen rooms were added on to the building as a South Wing, creating a division between the elementary and high school. The new three-story brick building had thirty classrooms, an auditorium, a cafeteria and a library.

Mr. M.W. Aiken was principal of both schools until 1942. In 1942, the high school enrollment was 731 students, while the elementary school had 863 students. The high school had grades eight through eleven with 27 teachers. In the first class, 29 students graduated. The elementary school had seven grades and 20 teachers. The library was equipped with 3,017 books. Washington School burned in the fall of 1939. The fire was seen by Mrs. Yeargin from her porch, and she was able to alert the fire department.

RICHARD B. HARRISON LIBRARY

In February 1935, a meeting was held at Christ Church to discuss establishing a library for the Negro population. Those involved included Mayor George Iseley, representatives from the North Carolina Library Commission, the North Carolina Department of Public Instruction and others.

As of that meeting, the decision was made to operate this library as an independent entity rather than a branch of the white public library. The mayor agreed to request a city appropriation of $2,500 toward the effort but requested that the Negro community raise funds to supplement this money.

The slogan for fundraising was "a dollar and a book." Between funds raised from businesses, personal gifts and proceeds of special concerts and entertainment, the Negro community raised $466.86 toward the establishment of the library. The county appropriated $750. There was enough money raised for the first location of the library to be at 135 East Hargett Street in the Delany Building. The assets on opening included 890 books, many of which were donated as part of the fundraiser.

The library opened on November 12, 1935. Mollie Huston Lee was chosen as the librarian. According to an interview with one of her staff members, she was considered a "go-getter." She received an AB degree from Howard University in 1929 and was the first Negro to receive a scholarship to the Columbia University School of Library Science as of 1934. She was the librarian at Shaw University from 1930 to 1935.

At Lee's request, the library was named after Richard B. Harrison. He was born in London, Ontario, on September 28, 1864. He was the son of runaway slaves. He worked as a farmhand, waiter, bellboy, Pullman porter, police investigator, elocutionist and drama teacher. Harrison was the drama instructor at North Carolina A&T College. While in Harlem looking for players for an amateur production of *The Merchant of Venice*, he was persuaded to take on the role of "De Lawd" in the all-Negro cast of *The Green Pastures*. After serving in this role for 1,659 performances, Harrison suffered a stroke. He died on March 14, 1935.

The common goal of the library staff was to make it "a community center around which all worthwhile activities in the city can revolve." Patrons of the library included adults, children and white people who were in business in the downtown area. Lee encouraged the attraction of young readers in order to make lifetime readers out of them. In this vein, she created story hours and organized boys' and girls' reading clubs, as well as vacation reading clubs. She also found ways to encourage teachers to use the library facilities.

- She made a miniature model of the library to illustrate its use and the use of books in Negro classrooms.
- When a book was ordered for the children's section, she also purchased another copy and placed it in a back room for teachers' use.
- She took books to schools to help form small classroom libraries.

In 1939, a bookmobile was borrowed from the North Carolina Library Commission. This was a test for two months to see if there was a need for additional service. After ascertaining that the service was needed, the county commissioners purchased one bookmobile to be used by both the white and Black libraries. Richard B. Harrison Library used it for eight days a month, and Olivia Raney Library used it for twelve days a month. Because of growing demand in the rural part of the county for library service, two bookmobiles were purchased in 1947.

The original library in the Delany Building rapidly became overcrowded. However, the library was unable to move until July 1948. At that time, it moved to the old Koontz Furniture Home Store at 214 South Blount Street. This was a two-story building that the library board purchased. Lee fundraised for the building.

In the upstairs of the building were two rooms. The hallway was lined with periodicals. The Black collection of books that Lee had started were in one room. Nonfiction books were in another room. Most of the downstairs was for juvenile and young adult books, with a room for adult fiction.

In 1947, a branch of the Richard B. Harrison Library was started in Chavis Heights. A second branch was started in Washington Terrace in

1951. Service was also provided to patients at St. Agnes Hospital with a book truck. Monthly, the bookmobile left books at the Wake County tuberculosis sanitarium as well. Services for the blind included talking books that were provided through the Edward A. Johnson fund for the blind, as well as gatherings hosted for the blind inside the library.

Eventually, some services were provided through the bookmobile to the rural schools that had few books, no library or no librarian. Adult education was much more informal. Monthly conversations and discussion groups were held along with film forums and lectures from distinguished guests.

In 1970, the library was moved to its present location on New Bern Avenue. Not only was the Mollie Huston Lee Black book collection in this space, but there was room still for community meetings. Lee and her staff always upheld the original purpose for the library space—encouraging the love of reading and being a community space for all.

FIRE COMPANIES

Early Raleigh housed two Black fire companies. The first company was formed on January 27, 1869, and was called Fire Company Number 1. The company operated an 1851 Rumsey and Company "double-decker" hand engine. After having won a competition with the engine in 1870 at the tenth state fair, it was called the Victor Fire Company in newspaper reports.

The Victor Fire Company was chartered by the General Assembly on January 23, 1872. The incorporators for this volunteer fire company were James H. Jones, H.C. Jones, H.P. Buncombe, John William, W.B. Mitchell, Charles M. Hunter, Samuel Stewart and Sylvester Dunston. The incorporation papers may be found in North Carolina Private Laws 1871–72, chapter 48.

James H. Jones was elected foreman of the company after incorporation and retained that title until 1882. Born free in 1831, he worked various jobs but was not formally educated. He was a brick mason and plasterer but also hired himself out as a waiter and gentlemen's servant.

In 1862, Confederate President Jefferson Davis sent his family to Raleigh to stay to keep them safe. Mr. Jones was hired to serve the family in Raleigh and returned to Richmond with them. He served in the capacity of courier and coachman until the end of the Civil War. After returning to Raleigh, Jones was appointed head doorkeeper for the North Carolina Constitutional Convention. He was also appointed deputy sheriff of Wake County and held that post until 1876.

Left: Victor Fire Station, home of Victor Hand Pump Company. Corner of Hargett and Blount Streets (1897–1913). There are no Black firemen in the photo. *The Albert Barden Collection, State Archives of North Carolina.*

Below: Oak City Blues, Black militia (circa 1884), at North Carolina Exposition. This group was authorized by General Assembly in 1868 and organized in 1876. *State Archives of North Carolina.*

The Victor Fire Company was housed in Metropolitan Hall at the back of the original City Market. This long two-story building was between Fayetteville and Wilmington Streets. Town Hall was also located there. A second Black company of firefighters was also housed in the hall. The Bucket and Ladder Company was organized on September 11, 1872. It was chartered by the General Assembly on February 28, 1873. The incorporators were A.L. Gorham, J.W. Winston, J.W. Butler, Ephraim Johnston, G.E. Lane and others. The Bucket and Ladder Company used a hand-pulled truck as of May 19, 1876. According to City of Raleigh minutes dated January 8, 1892, the board of alderman accepted a recommendation from the fire committee, and this company was disbanded.

By March 1891, the Victor Company moved from Metropolitan Hall to the former quarters of the Phoenix Chemical Company, a white fire company. This building was at the corner of Davie and Salisbury Streets. After a devastating fire that burned this location, killing two horses and damaging fire apparatus, the company moved into new quarters at 135 East Hargett Street, a two-story brick station.

The Victor Fire Company, about forty in number, wore uniforms consisting of black pants, red shirts trimmed in blue, black belts and blue leather hats trimmed to match the rest of their uniforms. Raleigh's fire department was originally a collection of private fire companies that operated under a fire chief appointed by the city. The volunteers in each company used equipment that was either privately owned or the city purchased it. By December 23, 1912, a fully paid fire department was created, and on March 7, 1913, the Victor Fire Company, along with the remaining volunteer companies, were declared out of commission. There would be no other Black firefighters in Raleigh until fifty years later.

RECREATION

Although life was difficult, there was time for recreation in the communities. Baseball was a sport that was commonplace among both Black and white people. If an ad or signboard was seen advertising a game coming to town and the word "grand" was included, that was a euphemism for a Black team, understood by both Blacks and whites.

During Reconstruction, there is mention in local newspapers of colored baseball teams. In 1897, there was an ad for a game played by the Raleigh Swiftfeet. In 1889, a *News & Observer* article shared information of an upcoming game, ending with, "Raleigh always wins." Finally, in 1904, there was a short notice about a game being played by the Raleigh Hard Sluggers at the Old Fairgrounds.

Games were usually played at the Old Fairgrounds. A 1904 article corroborates Howard Pullen's statement in an interview for *Culture Town*, when he talks about the cost of the games being prohibitive to watch for Blacks, so he and other youngsters peeked through the knot holes in the fence. The article says that "coloreds watched, sitting on the fence, peeping through cracks in the fence, taking reserved seats on the top of hardy trees surrounding the park."

Old State Fairgrounds Stone Marker. This site served as a military training camp in the Civil War, a racetrack and a baseball park. It is at the corner of Tarboro Road and Lincoln Court. *City of Raleigh.*

1920s

During the 1920s, we find mention of teams in Raleigh such as the Raleigh Black Star Line, named after Marcus Garvey's freight company.

- The original Raleigh Grays played in 1919 and 1920. They were owned by a man from South Carolina, but the roster included Allen Olmstead, James Yancey, "Red" McCoy, C.O. Watkins, Taylor (full name unknown), Willard Perry, Fred Williams and Charles "Doll" Haywood, who eventually started Raleigh Funeral Home, now Haywood Funeral Home.
- The Raleigh Tar Heels played in 1920 and 1921. Their star pitcher was Eulace Harrington, and his playing ability was compared to "Satchel" Paige.
- Raleigh also had a team called the South Park Hornets. They were managed by Joe Watkins and had players including Floyd "Deacon" Jones, "Jumpin'" Joe Wiggins, "Skink" Browning,

Elijah Austin, W.A. "Pete" Wilder and Aaron "Rabbit" Shaw. This team was owned by a railroad man named Will Brevard from South Carolina.

Railroad men, who had better-paying jobs than most men who weren't college-educated, sponsored several of the baseball teams financially. Others were sponsors as well.

Twilight League Sponsors*		
Name	**Job**	**Team**
Ike Massenburg	Joe P. White & Sons	Fourth Ward
Hubert Toms	U.S. Postal Carrier	Fourth Ward
Connie Cagle	Railroad	East Raleigh
Tom Scales	Railroad	Idlewild
Andrew Parish	State College (NCSU)	Method
Bill Wilcox	Teacher	Method
Will Brevard	Railroad	South Park
Jimmy Page	State Department	West Raleigh

*Called registered sponsors

There were several baseball leagues during the early 1930s, both Black and white. The Twilight League was created in Raleigh and was the brainchild of Aaron "Skink" Browning. He attended Shaw University and was considered a standout catcher on the South Park Hornet team. "Browning was quite a back stop. He also played for the 1928 Wilmington, Delaware Potomacs with future Hall of Fame third baseman William 'Judy' Johnson," according to an article by Bijan C. Bayne in the book *Baseball in the Carolinas: 25 Lessons on the States' Hardball Heritage*. On his return to the area, he coached in Statesville, North Carolina.

The Twilight League was so named because their games started between four and five o'clock every evening. The teams played by baseball rules. If a player signed up with one team, he stayed with that team unless he was traded. There were very few trades because "everybody was afraid of everybody else."

W.A. "Pete" Wilder said in his *Culture Town* interview that a cartoonist thought they were the best organized Black league in the world. Once the season began, there was a game every day at each location. They were community teams. However, "fellows would leave places like Rocky Mount to come play in this league. People would keep them in the communities and give them room and board and some money." The teams played each other in three-game series starting the Friday before Labor Day, ending with a doubleheader on Labor Day. Any money that was made was divided between the two teams.

There was no admission charge because they were playing during the Depression, and no one had money. People forgot they didn't have money, forgot they were out of work, enjoyed the ballgame and went home happy.

Twilight League Fields Played On	
Team Name	**Field Played On**
Fourth Ward	Back of Washington School
East Raleigh	no known information
Idlewild	St. Augustine's
Lincoln Park	St. Augustine's
Method	back of Berry O'Kelly Training School
South Park	Buckeye Field
West Raleigh	Red Diamond

1930s: Raleigh Grays

The Raleigh Grays were a professional team developed by W.A. "Pete" Wilder. He pulled the best of the local teams to develop this one, which began in 1937. The team played at Shaw Alumni Field. According to Wilder, "you got to have a winner in this town or you can forget it."

Financially, the teams played for a percentage of the gate charged above the field's rent, which was anywhere from $0.40 to $0.60 admission per game. There were three days of games played. On the first two days, team members received no money. Money was borrowed from park rent on day one to bring the team members to play the doubleheader on day two. Out of the first three games that were played, team members made $1.00 to $1.50.

The Black teams made sure they could accommodate or see more white people than just Blacks at the games. White attendees would bring their own chairs. Attendance for weekday games, when played at Chavis, would be anywhere from two thousand to twenty-five hundred people and three thousand to thirty-five hundred people on Fridays and Saturdays. By the 1939–40 season, the Grays had moved to the new Chavis Park field.

According to Wilder, white baseball clubs had trouble existing. Wilder pulled attractions from New York for the Black team, including the use of bookies. He also had agreements in place that if teams wouldn't play the Grays, they couldn't play any teams in the eastern part of the state. (There were similar arrangements for the Asheville team regarding the teams in the western part of the state as well.)

One of the attractions that came to Raleigh was the House of David team from Pottsville, Pennsylvania, owned by Sean Potts. The team traveled with their own lights, and it was the first time the Grays had played under lights. After that game, the white baseball team, the Raleigh Cavs, wanted to play the Grays in a series. Charlie Chim pitched for the Cavs but was only able to last five innings. The teams had originally agreed that the Grays would not put their best ace (or pitcher) in until the last game. The Grays team members usually got forty dollars every time they played. When the Raleigh Cavs played their series for their league championship, they only got sixty dollars for the entire series. The financial difference was keen.

1940s: RALEIGH TIGERS

"Pete" Wilder left Raleigh for New York and returned in the early 1940s. He was approached by Arthur Dove, who had money and wanted a baseball team. From this partnership, the Raleigh Tigers were started in 1946. They were barnstormers and traveled east of the Mississippi. Barnstorming meant that although the teams traveled, they were not formal leagues. These were exhibition games, set up by the players, owners or independent promoters. Often, like in the early vaudeville touring entertainment days, they played in barns or hastily created fields. In the East, games were generally played between the end of the World Series and the onset of winter.

Dove worked with the LA Dodgers, training and trading players to that team. Team members were traded elsewhere as well. They included Pete

Smith, who went to the Cincinnati Cardinals. Charlie Neal went from Brooklyn to the Giants to Cincinnati. Dan Bankhead played for Brooklyn. Wes Covington and Milt Smith also played for the Tigers before being traded forward. The Raleigh Tigers played until the early 1960s.

Buckeye Field

Outside of the fields listed in the chart on page 75, there were three other main fields used. Buckeye Field was used in the Twilight League by the South Park team, as well as in the 1930s. The Buckeye Mill owned land at the end of the 1300 block of South Bloodworth Street, leading into the street beyond the old Providence Holiness Church. The men who wanted to play ball decided to fix it in order to play there.

Shaw Alumni Field/Shaw Park

Another field was the Shaw Alumni Field or Shaw Park. It was located in the space where the Student Union and two residential halls are today. This area was called Faculty Row at the time due to the faculty housing situated on South Blount Street. The field was completed by Calvin Lightner. Wilder called it a "hand-to-mouth affair."

Piedmont League Ball Park

The Piedmont League Ball Park was located between Edenton Street and Tarboro Road crossing over to Martin Street and going down to Pettigrew Street. It was situated on what we know today as Lincoln Court. The ballpark was across the street from the Confederate Old Soldiers Home that was at the site of the Old Fairgrounds. (In 1910, this area had no streets, electricity or running water. There were only dirt paths, and two cars couldn't pass on the path at the same time.)

Chavis Park

Chavis Park was built on some of the Watson Lands discussed in a later section of the book. According to a letter written by attorney Curtis A. Weathers, dated July 18, 1935, he worked with city commissioners and others ("white and colored") "to advocate for a bill authorizing the State to lease to the city certain unused lands in the Eastern section of our city for a period of twenty-five years for the purpose of a Negro park. This bill was enacted in the law and is shown as Chapter 251 of the Public Laws of 1935."

While Raleigh was already in possession of Pullen Park, which had been gifted to the city by Richard Stanhope Pullen, the facilities were not allowed for use by the Black population outside of the grassy areas. Building a park with recreational facilities allowed separate but equal to continue in the broadest of terms. This attitude is alluded to in several letters of support to the mayor and city commissioners, but none phrased it in the exact terms as does Attorney Weathers. He goes on to state:

> *Several considerations occur in support of this project: first, if federal funds can be obtained to develop this park, it will provide a valuable asset to our city. We now possess adequate park facilities for white people at Pullen Park. Obviously, there should be adequate and proper provision for a suitable park for the colored race. I think that the public park for Negroes would be of infinite value in affording the proper means for recreation of Negro children. In this connection it should serve in solving, in some measure, the question of juvenile delinquency among the colored race. Besides, recreational facilities for our colored citizens are most advisable and justified. Furthermore, it seems to me that having a suitable public park for Negroes in the eastern section of our city would remove the necessity of attempting to provide adequate facilities for both races at Pullen Park. Thus, Pullen Park could be devoted to recreational activities for white people solely, which seems a wise course.*

The thoughts he states, in particular about the question of juvenile delinquency among the colored race, were echoed in letters of support from attorney William Y. Bickett; Paul A. Daniel, superintendent of Raleigh Public Schools; and Mrs. Hubert Young, executive director of the Wake County Chapter of the American Red Cross. It is amazing that each of these letters mentioned that same point in their urge for a park for Negroes and federal funds to pay for it.

All of the aforementioned letters are dated July 18, 1935. The Statement of Allotment Detail for the Park Work Project and Payroll was approved on November 25, 1935, with an estimated completion date of June 30, 1936. The description of the project says that it "provides recreational facilities near the center of the Negro population and midway between two Negro colleges. Includes swimming pool, baseball diamond, tennis courts, etc."

Pete Wilder stated that once the park was opened, it would attract twenty-five to thirty busloads of people every day from all over. The park was a novelty because there was no other facility in the Mid-Atlantic region that was a new, well-planned, fun attraction for the Black population, and it had an Olympic-sized pool.

Many Black teachers worked there during the summer for additional pay. A few students worked in areas like the pools and the carousel. According to Wilder, who worked in recreation for the city, all types of recreation were provided, including baseball, basketball, softball, tennis, horseshoes, checkers, hopscotch and drop switch. Swimming and the carousel or merry-go-round were also available. Many people came to spend a family day at the park. There were also concession stands at one point.

After Chavis Heights apartments were built, also using federal Works Progress Administration funds, parents felt safe sending their children to the park for recreation to be looked after either by adults at work or older siblings who were also in the park.

Pete Wilder stated that there were no helpers when the park first opened. He had to be at work early enough to mark off fields and get them ready on his own. He also had to account for all recreation, whether active or passive. Jack Knapp, of the National Recreation Association, visited the park to see how it was run and was impressed enough to return to his work and talk about it.

POLITICS

While Black men worked hard in the business arena, they were also deeply involved in politics. Most of those who were registered to vote were Republicans, just as Black people were across most of the country. Obviously, this was in large part due to that being the party of President Abraham Lincoln. The members of the Democratic Party, particularly in the South, were well known for their unyielding stance on race and their continuing enmity for those who had been formerly enslaved.

This chart shows the political activity of many of the Raleigh and Wake County Black residents during the period after slavery ended. Where known, for the census of 1870, the value of the property that was owned by the individual is shown, as well as other information gathered.

REPUBLICAN MEETINGS.

The Republicans held two meetings last night. They wer eattended almost entirely by negroes. In the Third ward they met in the Royal Knights Hall; in the Second ward the pow-wow was in the vicinity of the Cox Memorial church, on "Hungry Neck," in a negro store. Thursday night the First warders met. They held forth at Thos. Lyon's have on Northwest strete, near the Episcopal church.

The Republican primaries have been called for next Thursday night. The Republican city convention will met Friday night. The convention will be held at the court house or Metropolitan hall. Cir- .   . ore issued ʀ r fɪ ʀʏ by Jim ... i . ꞏe ꞏ ꞏ the prima-

This Republican meeting notice mentions Hungry Neck. *From the* News and Observer, *April 17, 1897.*

OFFICE HOLDERS AND GOVERNMENT STAFF

Name	Year Served	Office/Position Held	1870 Census, Real Estate	1870 Census, Personal Property	Occupation	Other Information
Adams, Jesse P.	1868	justice of the peace, appointed by Governor W.W. Holden	$270.00	$170	farmer	
	1868	Wake County Board of Assessors				
Baker, James	1895–97	Raleigh alderman	$600	$100	grocer	mulatto, educated
Brodie, George W.	1866	presiding elder, Raleigh District AME Church			minister, abolitionist	educated, born free
	1867	Supervisor of Voter Registration Board, appointment				
	1868	Freedman Savings Bank, cashier of local branch				
	1868	director of the State Insane Asylum, appointed by General Assembly				
	1869	supervisor of charitable institutions				

Name	Year Served	Office/Position Held	1870 Census, Real Estate	1870 Census, Personal Property	Occupation	Other Information
Brown, John H.	1881-2	Raleigh alderman			carpenter	mulatto, educated
Caswell, John R.	1865–56	Freedmen's Convention, delegate			teacher, mason, storekeeper	mulatto, educated
	1870–72	Wake County commissioner				
Cole, Reuben	1885–87	Raleigh alderman			grocer	mulatto, educated
	1888–89	Raleigh alderman				
Craven, Simon	1868	Raleigh policeman				
Crosson, Robert	1868	Raleigh policeman				
Dunstan, M. Nelson	1885–87	Raleigh alderman			barber	educated, born free
Dunston, Norfleet	1868	Wake County magistrate	$700	$300	shoemaker	born free, educated
	1868–69; 1877–83	Raleigh alderman				instrumental in improving City Cemetery

Name	Year Served	Office/Position Held	1870 Census, Real Estate	1870 Census, Personal Property	Occupation	Other Information
	1872	Raleigh tax receiver				
	1872	registrar, justice of the peace				
Ellison, Stewart	1868	New Hanover County Board of Assessors; magistrate			commercial construction; grocery store owner	born slave, self-educated, hired to work in Raleigh construction including insane asylum (1852–54)
	1869	Raleigh Board of City Commissioners (14 years)				
	1870–80	House of Representatives for Wake County				opposed beating of convicts
	1880s; 1890s	county jailor and janitor at courthouse and post office				
Farrar, Albert	1869–1871	Raleigh alderman	$1,000		blacksmith	born free, 1814, educated

Name	Year Served	Office/Position Held	1870 Census, Real Estate	1870 Census, Personal Property	Occupation	Other Information
	1868–69	Wake County magistrate and constable				
Goins, Bennett B.	1882–83	Raleigh alderman			teacher	educated
Hamlin, James	1883–84	Raleigh alderman			saloonkeeper, druggist	mulatto, educated
	1897–1901 (3 terms)	Raleigh alderman				
Harris, Andrew J.	1887–89				porter	educated
Harris, James H.	1865	president of State Equal Rights League	$4,000	$1,000		born free, dark mulatto, literate
	1865	delegate to Freedmen's Convention				1863, raised Black soldiers in Indiana for 28th U.S. Colored Troops
	1866	chair, Colored Education Convention				1865, teacher for colored people for New England Freedmen's Aid Society

Name	Year Served	Office/Position Held	1870 Census, Real Estate	1870 Census, Personal Property	Occupation	Other Information
	1867	Union League organizer				editor and publisher, *Raleigh Gazette* and *Raleigh NC Republican*
	1868	Wake County representative in Constitutional Convention				
	1868–70; 1873	House of Representatives for Wake County				
	1872–74	senator for Wake County				
		justice of the peace				
		Wake County assessor				
	1868, 1875–78, 1887–90	Board of City Commissioners				
		superintendent of the Deaf, Dumb, Blind School for Colored				

Name	Year Served	Office/Position Held	1870 Census, Real Estate	1870 Census, Personal Property	Occupation	Other Information
	1868, 1872, 1876	delegate for Republican National Convention				
	1883	U.S. deputy tax collector				
Hoover, Charles W.	1879–85	Raleigh alderman				
	1895–97 (7 terms)	Wake County legislator			huckster; bar owner	mulatto, educated
Hunter, Armenius	1883–84	Raleigh alderman			box mail collector	mulatto, educated
Hunter, Wesley/ Willie	1868	Raleigh policeman				
Johnson, Edward A.	1893–95; 1897–99 (2 terms)	Raleigh alderman			lawyer, dean of Shaw Law School	mulatto, educated
Jones, Henry C.	1872–74	Wake County commissioner			brick mason, teacher	born 1836, literate
	1875–76	Raleigh alderman				

Name	Year Served	Office/Position Held	1870 Census, Real Estate	1870 Census, Personal Property	Occupation	Other Information
Jones, James H.	1861–65	coachman, personal servant, confidential courier for Jefferson Davis			brick mason, plasterer, tailor, gentleman's servant	born free, mulatto, literate
	1865–66	delegate, Freedmen's Convention				1880s, worked as contractor constructing waterworks and street railroads
	1865–66	official of Union League				
	1868	head doorkeeper of Freedmen's Convention				
	1868–77	deputy sheriff of Wake County				
	1869–82	fireman, Victory Fire Company, Raleigh Fire Department				
	1873–89	Raleigh alderman				
	1876	helped to organize first Black militia company				

Name	Year Served	Office/Position Held	1870 Census, Real Estate	1870 Census, Personal Property	Occupation	Other Information
Lockhart, Hardy	1866	delegate, Freedmen's Convention	$1,500	$300	carpenter, undertaker	1807–84, slave, mulatto, literate
	1868–69	Raleigh town commissioner; New Hanover county assessor				1820s, worked as servant to Raleigh cabinetmaker for 40 years
	1875	Magistrate				
	1868, 1873	justice of the peace				
Lunn, Bryan	1868	assistant to Raleigh police chief				
Mathews, W.H.	1887–89	Raleigh alderman	$1,100		brick mason	literate
Mitchell, William	1878–79	Raleigh alderman	$325		well digger; brick mason	literate
Morgan, Wilson	1870–92	House of Representatives for Wake County	$1,000	$600	brick mason, blacksmith, minister	born free, mulatto, literate
Raynor, Samuel	1872–74	Wake County commissioner			landscape gardener	

Name	Year Served	Office/Position Held	1870 Census, Real Estate	1870 Census, Personal Property	Occupation	Other Information
Ricks, Virgil	1873–74; 1879–80	Raleigh alderman			provision dealer/ storekeeper, restaurateur	mulatto, literate
Roberts, Nicholas F.	1885–87	Raleigh alderman			college professor	literate
Robinson, B.J.	1889–99 (5 terms)	Raleigh alderman			grocer	literate
Tate, Alfred	1891–93	Raleigh alderman			clerk	mulatto, literate
Williams, Charles	1891–1901	Raleigh alderman			principal, college instructor/ Deaf, Dumb, Blind School	literate
Young, James H.	1883–84	Raleigh alderman			clerk in Revenue Department	mulatto, literate

*Alderman, Raleigh City Council, Raleigh Board of Commissioners and Raleigh Town Commissioners are the same office.

89

Part III

NEIGHBORHOODS

OBERLIN VILLAGE (FREE PEOPLE)

Oberlin Village was originally located on Hillsborough Road, which led northward out of Raleigh, crossing the land of Fendel Beavers and the farm of Lewis W. Peck. The area went past Paul Cameron's land and the Boylan land going toward the gristmill in the Crabtree Creek area.

From the fire station and Park Avenue, Oberlin Road stretched twelve blocks to Colonial Road in the 1940s. We're told that included two churches, a public school, a cemetery, a hall and one hundred residences. Then the area spread westward through intersections with lateral streets. Crossing that added seventy-five additional homes. The population in 1948 was about one thousand people. One of the original inhabitants of Oberlin was Thomas Williams. His home was at the corner of Oberlin Road and Clark Avenue.

In 1858, a sixteen-acre parcel of land was sold to Jesse Pettiford (1792–1870) on the new road from Raleigh to Hillsborough. He paid $160 for this land. The street was renamed Oberlin Road in the early 1870s. Jesse Pettiford worked for the Mordecais as a tenant farmer and eventually saved enough money to buy the land. He was a free mulatto born in the state of Virginia.

In 1868, the land price per acre in Wake County was approximately $5.70. Lewis Peck sold his farm after subdividing it into equal-sized one-and-three-quarter-acre lots. Here are some of the prices paid for land in Oberlin as well as the names of many of the new owners:

Oberlin Village Land Purchasers (Partial List)		
Name	Price Paid	Acreage
Jesse Pettiford	$160.00	160 acres
Thomas Williams, carpenter		
317 Oberlin Road	$90.00	1.75 acres
Norfleet Jeffreys	$95.00	1.9 acres
Henry Jones	$50.00	1 acre
Seth Nowell, drayman	$43.75	1.75 acres
Willis M. Graves, Justice of the Peace		
Andrew Andrews, Wake County Negro who drew Confederate pension for his labor building the earth breastworks around the city of Raleigh, March 1865		
M. Smith	Richard Shepherd	Robert Williams
Albert Williams	A.J. Webb	Thomas Higgs
Andrew Hinton	N.C. Dunston	Allen Haywood
Balam Shepherd	Alonzo Peebles	Haynes Clark
Thomas Crosson	Henderson Poole	James Shepard
Henry Williams	Willis Wilder	Alfred Vincent
John James	Grandison Turner	Wilson Copeland
John Dickerson	Alfred and Sarah Williams	John Flagg
Simon Barker	Betsy Hinton	

There were three companies that were chartered to help provide building loans to purchase land and build homes in the Oberlin Village. They are the North Carolina Land Company, the National Freedmen's Savings and Trust Association and the Raleigh Cooperative Land and Building Association. (These are discussed in detail in a prior chapter.)

The Wake County sheriff, Timothy F. Lee, was a Union soldier from Brooklyn. He was considered a carpetbagger (a person from the northern states who went to the South after the Civil War to profit from the

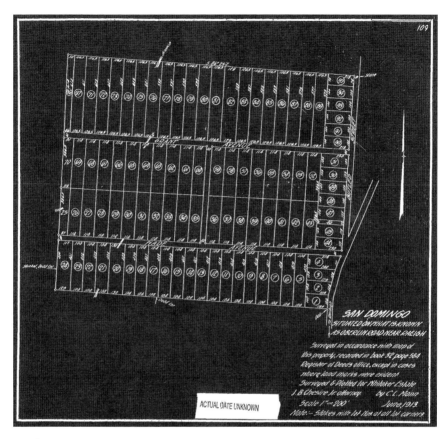

San Domingo plat map showing street names and plotted parcels of land in Oberlin Village. *Wake County Register of Deeds.*

Reconstruction). Sheriff Lee and James Harris were considered "promoters" of Oberlin Village. In 1869, the William Boylan land was sold by court order. This land was north of Peck's farmland. The sheriff bought part of a tract of land for $1,626.50. Five acres upland was purchased by W.H. Morgan and the Cooperative Land Company.

Sheriff Lee subdivided the thirty-four acres that he purchased into lots and sold them to Negroes at low prices. Dr. Albert Smith, St. Mary's Junior College official, helped many of the servants at the school purchase land. In 1870, the Whitaker land was subdivided and platted as San Domingo, which was considered part of Oberlin Village.

Oberlin Village/San Domingo Street Names		
Street Name	**Reason for Name**	**Name Change (If Applicable)**
Grant Avenue	President Ulysses Grant	
Wade Avenue	Senator Wade of Ohio, abolitionist	
Butler Street	General B.F. Butler, controversial Union general who refused to uphold the Fugitive Slave Act	Changed to Chester Drive
Baez Street	President Buenaventura Baez of Haiti, who negotiated a treaty for annexation of Santo Domingo by U.S. in 1869, which was not ratified	
Stafford Avenue	Gaston Stafford, longtime custodian of State Fairgrounds	
Roberts Lane	Reverend N.F. Roberts, professor at Shaw University and last Negro member to serve on the three-member Wake County Board of Education	Changed from Fourth Street
Barber Street	Well-known Negro family	Changed to Van Dyke

There are many stories about where the name Oberlin came from. In an August 8, 1948 *News and Observer* article by Willis Briggs, he states, "The oldest inhabitants say it was named after Jean Frederick Oberlin (1746–1826), the father of orphanages, who spent his long life for uplift of the degraded. Oberlin College was named after him." A young man from Raleigh named Copeland, who died in the John Brown raid, and James Harris both attended Oberlin College. Nicknames for the Oberlin community have included "Save Rent," "Peck's Place" and "Morganton" (for Benjamin Morgan).

On the 1880 tax list, Oberlin Village residents possessed land more than in any other section of Raleigh. There were ninety Black landowners with

THE OBERLIN PROCESSION.—About 80 negroes from Oberlin—San Domingo—Save-Rent—Morganton—marched into the city yesterday with banners-flying and drums beating. They march ed to the polls deposited their ballots for Grant as two thirds of the crowd thought.

We are told that this organized band of voters, after parading the streets, huzzahing and yelling as so many demons, the like of which was never before known in this community, halted in front of the box and complained very bitterly of not being able to vote at once in a body. The procession was no doubt organized for a purpose, by designing men, and though it failed to either intimidate honest voters or grind any more for the Radical ticket, yet such a proceeding should be denounced by all good citizens as infamous and disreputable.

This image shows the importance of political equity for Black citizens as members of Oberlin community march to the polls to cast votes in the presidential election. *From the* Raleigh News, *August 3, 1872.*

between $200 and $500 worth of real estate. The major landowner was John Turner, who owned six parcels valued at $2,850.

According to the Briggs article, there were all types of houses and designs in the community, and they could have been any of the houses in Raleigh's white neighborhoods. Primarily, the homes were one- and two-story frame houses. Several spacious homes showed the growing middle-class stature of the residents.

In 1891, ten years after Oberlin was incorporated, the village had stores, a Baptist and AME church, and two schools (Oberlin Graded and Latta University). In 1900, Oberlin Road ran from Hillsborough Street to Glenwood Avenue and to Beaver Dam Branch from as far away as Brooks Avenue.

OBERLIN GRADED SCHOOL

Some of the teachers at the Oberlin School were Kittie Richardson, Fannie Peace, Nanny O'Kelley and Julia Ames.

Top: Oberlin Graded School. This red brick school was built in 1916 by the citizens of the community for the education of their children. *State Archives of North Carolina.*

Bottom: Report on Oberlin Graded School's closing exercises by Principal Charles N. Hunter. *Charles N. Hunter Scrapbook, Duke University Papers.*

LATTA UNIVERSITY

NOTICE.

Latta Unsversity will be closed during the Christmas holidays for all the session for the purpose of rebuilding the buildings that were consumed by fire last May, and also additional buildings. The University is located in the village of Oberlin, N. C., one and one-half miles west of the capitol building in the city. The location is the very best for a school, being out of the busy city, but within easy reach by means of the electric street cars. It is enough to say, that there has not been a single case of serious illness since the establishment of the school. Each dormitory is heated by stoves and hearths, so every necessary comfort is secured. The terms are very reasonable—$7 50 per month. Those desiring to reduce their expenses by work will be taken at the lowest possible rates: young men $6 40 per month ; young women $5.40 per month; day students $1 per month. A small incidental fee will be charged.

The school will reopen on the 7th day of October, 1897. Our purpose is to make it one of the largest schools in the South for the race. Law and Medicine will be added. The institution is wholly non-sectarian in its religious instruction or influence. Yet earnest attention will be given to Bible study, applying its truths to daily life and conduct, that a thorough Christian character may be obtained. It is open to all students of either sex. None but competent teachers will be employed.

For further information, address the President, Rev. M. L. Latta, D. D.

I will leave for the North and Europe the latter part of December or the first of January, and will return time enough to have buildings completed by the reopening of the school. The University will contain eight buildings.

dec. 5—6 m.

An ad for Latta University in Oberlin Village, founded by Reverend Morgan L. Latta. *From the* Gazette, *April 10, 1897.*

Latta University was founded by Reverend Morgan L. Latta. He was born in 1853 as a slave on the Cameron estate, the largest plantation east of the Mississippi. His determination to be educated pushed him to persevere through circumstances that would have stopped others. Reverend Latta graduated from Shaw University in spite of poverty and poor health. His fortitude spurred his teaching career, which spanned almost twenty years before he became a salesman.

Latta University was established in part to prove that "a member of the colored race could do anything...regardless of color or previous condition of servitude." According to Reverend Latta's autobiography, *The History of My Life and Work*, the school was able to accommodate more than fourteen hundred students. He stated that there were twenty-three buildings on the campus, and three had been lost to fires.

The main building of Latta University was on property that was purchased in 1891. The founding date of the school is 1892. He formed the university to "solve the race problem." The school was situated on close to three hundred acres of land near Beaver Dam Branch, close to Brooks Avenue up to what is now Oberlin Road. The school was open to both male and female students. Students were encouraged to board on campus, where they were part of either the normal school, the industrial department or the night school.

In order to help with expenses of the school, Reverend Latta traveled throughout the United States and Europe to raise funds to keep the school open. To offset payments required from students, he also worked other jobs to help defray the expenses of running a boarding school.

Dormitories at Latta University. *From* The History of My Life and Work, *autobiography by Reverend M.L. Latta.*

The City of Raleigh began to annex the land in Oberlin Village in the late 1920s. The street paving assessments, taxes and the Depression led to loss of land for some of the residents. Quite a bit of land was sold at the courthouse.

WILSON TEMPLE UNITED METHODIST CHURCH

In 1865, a group of Oberlin residents came together and founded a Methodist Episcopal church. (Original records have been lost, probably due to damage to the church from Hurricane Hazel in 1954.) Wilson W. Morgan, one of the original land purchasers, donated a portion of property for construction of the building, which was subsequently named Wilson Chapel in his honor. The church is still on the original grounds at 1023 Oberlin Road, although it has been rebuilt and remodeled. The original wooden building housed a sanctuary with a balcony and a basement. The brick structure is now a Raleigh historic site.

The pastor noted in 1873–74 was M.G. Groom. While two lists exist showing membership of twenty-four and thirty-six names, the first official membership document of 1890 has a list of fifty-five persons. Officers listed in 1885 include L.B. Hinton, Robert Hogan, Willie M. Graves, Larkin S. Hall, Frank Thornton, Jacob Merritt, A.W. Morgan, Anderson Person, O.

Curtis, J.D. Morgan, R.L. Pettiford, Willie Haywood, Charles Lockhart, John Mallory, J.F. Flagg and others. The name was changed to Wilson Temple United Methodist Church as part of a denominational change and merger. Many descendants of the original families still belong to the church.

OBERLIN BAPTIST CHURCH

In 1878, Reverend Plummer T. Hall organized a "community church" on Wade Avenue in the 2000 block (where the ramp from Wade Avenue exits to Oberlin Road today) close to the present Jaycee Park site. The church moved to the 1300 block of Oberlin Road and was called First Baptist Church of Oberlin. In 1885, the church again moved, this time to 806 Oberlin Road, its present location, and the name became Hall's Chapel. Mount Moriah Baptist Church was situated in the 600 block of Oberlin Road. On July 6, 1912, the two churches merged to form what is now Oberlin Baptist Church.

JAMES H. HARRIS

James Henry Harris was considered the "Black warhorse" of Raleigh. He was born in Granville County in 1832. At the age of eight, he was apprenticed to learn the carpentry trade. After his apprenticeship, he opened a shop in Raleigh. He was mostly self-educated other than the apprenticeship, until he attended school in Oberlin, Ohio. In 1862, he traveled to Canada, Liberia and Sierra Leone. In 1863, he was commissioned by Governor Levi Morton of Indiana to raise the Twenty-Eighth Regiment of U.S. Colored Troops. In 1865, he returned to Raleigh as a teacher for the New England Freedmen's Aid Society.

He was a state and national politician from 1865 into the 1880s. In 1865, he was elected as a delegate to the North Carolina Freedmen's Convention. He urged moderation, reconciliation with whites and education for Blacks at the time. In 1869, he was president of the National Convention of Colored Men and pushed for Black rights. Eventually, he changed his position and pushed for education for Blacks, an end to legal discrimination, prison reform, aid to mechanics and laborers, protection for women and debtors and care for orphans.

Harris was also chair of a delegation urging President Ulysses Grant to influence Congress to pass supplemental legislation securing equal rights for Blacks. In 1872, he was a presidential elector.

During Reconstruction, Harris was a charter member of the Republican Party and a delegate to the 1866 Constitutional Convention. He was a state legislator, serving two terms in the House of Representatives from 1868 to 1870. He was a member of the North Carolina Senate from 1872 to 1873. Locally, Harris served as a justice of the peace, a City of Raleigh assessor and a member of the city's Board of Aldermen in 1868, 1875 to 1878 and again from 1887 to 1890. He also served as the superintendent for the state's Deaf, Dumb and Blind Asylum for Colored.

Harris declined nomination for Congress. A couple of years later, he decided to run and was unsuccessful. He was appointed a U.S. deputy tax collector. He also edited and published the Raleigh *North Carolina Republican* and the *Raleigh Gazette* during the 1880s. James H. Harris was one of the original trustees for St. Ambrose Episcopal Church.

METHOD

Today, the Method community is located in West Raleigh between Hillsboro Street and Western Boulevard. According to an interview with Reverend Whalen Hogan for the book *Culture Town*, the land that his family owned, which was part of the original Method community, crossed Western Boulevard and ran out to the Gorman Street Extension.

General W.R. Cox, who was a Confederate veteran, sold part of his plantation in small plots to Blacks on easy purchase terms. In 1872, Lewis Mason and Isaac O'Kelly purchased sixty-nine acres three miles west of Raleigh from the general and his wife. The area was originally called "Save Rent," a colloquialism for Blacks moving from Raleigh to prevent having to pay high rent. Another nickname for the community was "Slabtown." This was because of the use of slabs cut from timber to build the houses there.

The acreage that was purchased was divided into large tracts and sold as home sites. The first houses were single-room log or slab cabins like pioneer dwellings. The first property owners who acquired sizable tracts of land were Lewis Atwater, Jerry Hogan, Merritt Wilder, Jane Wilder, Caroline Tilley, Lafayette Ligon, John Ligon and Arthur Hunter.

The residents had varied ways of earning a living, including farming, janitorial and construction work at State College, carpentry and seasonal day labor on plantations or farms. Women worked as domestics, as farm laborers, providing laundry services or doing odd jobs. The need for services to be provided in the community increased as the population of the area grew. This included the need for stores, churches, a school, a post office and a train stop.

Method community citizens on donation/subscription list, paid to Charles N. Hunter, from a ledger in his personal papers. *Charles N. Hunter Scrapbook, Duke University Papers.*

In an interview for the book *Culture Town*, Verde P. Washington talks about some of the businesses. She states, "Mr. Parrish had a store at the corner of Beryl Drive and Method Road. It was close to the Berry O'Kelly Training School. Students would come to the edge of the road, give their order for purchase and we would take things to them. The store sold fish that was purchased from the City Market. We also sold bunches of bananas, barrels of apples, candy, vegetables and Lassiter meal." The land that the store was on had been leased for ten years, but O'Kelly undercut the price on Washington's father and purchased the land. Washington's chores included chopping cotton and planting corn. The family also planted salad, which was sold to the Berry O'Kelly School. The family had eight students who boarded with them that they had to feed daily, so they fed them from their garden.

Mr. Wood had a store, and Berry O'Kelly worked in the store with him. Eventually, they were in partnership together. Wood sold his share to O'Kelly and moved to Oklahoma. The students from the Berry O'Kelly Training School bought ice cream, candy and shoes at the store.

Reverend Whalen Hogan's father farmed the two hundred acres of land that his grandfather, Jerry Hogan, purchased from Thomas Argo for forty dollars in the community. This is the land that ran to the end of the Gorman Street Extension. His grandmother, Janet, had a convenience store and sold cakes, candy and ice cream. Most of the residents who lived in Method worked at the university. The land that the Hogan family owned was considered down in the bottom from there to Beryl Road. The Method boundaries extended across what is now the Beltline to Brickhaven Drive near the back of the Arboretum.

According to Reverend Hogan, the neighbors all got along. They shared equipment if they needed it and farmed together. Most of the items that families needed were purchased at the Berry O'Kelly store. The Hogan family sold their property so the Gorman Street Extension could be created. Their family cemetery is at the bottom of the land that was sold.

According to Katie Jones, school was started after Christmas because the Black children had to stay home to harvest crops, as opposed to the white children for whom school started earlier in the fall. Her family owned six acres of land that her grandfather received when they were freed from slavery. Because Method was outside the city limits, they were not under the Raleigh Township School committee for many years.

Method's nickname was changed from "Slabtown" or "Save Rent" to "Mason Village" to recognize the leadership of Lewis Mason, who was the son of Jesse Mason. The name Mason Village was changed to Method by decision of the Southern Railroad Company. After acquiring the post office for the area, Berry O'Kelly was given a lifetime appointment as the postmaster. He was able to have the railroad stop to pick up mail. Furthermore, he was able to purchase freight and siding that he could sell, and passengers were able to board the train at that stop.

OAK CITY BAPTIST CHURCH

Oak City Baptist Church in Method was organized in 1873. It was built on a hill beside the cemetery that was located to its north. The church was named for the grove of oak trees on the grounds and is still located on its original site.

ST. JAMES AME CHURCH

In 1886, St. James AME Church was founded in Method. Berry O'Kelly was a steward of the church and collaborated with several other men to purchase land for it. It continues to stand on the same site.

BERRY O'KELLY TRAINING SCHOOL

Originally in Method, there was a one-room private-pay school in a log cabin that had a two-month term. The tuition for the two-month term was four dollars in 1871. That was replaced by a two-teacher school in 1873. In 1895, a new school was built on the site. This became part of the Berry O'Kelly Training School campus. This also served as the community school until 1914.

The Berry O'Kelly Training School was established in 1914. O'Kelly bought the land. He expanded the facilities and the curriculum of the

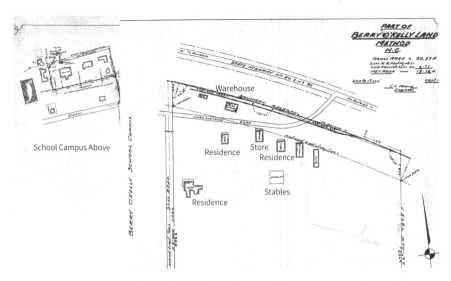

This property map of the famous Rosenwald-funded Berry O'Kelly Training School (Method) includes O'Kelly's warehouse, dormitories and other entrepreneurial ventures. *Wake County Register of Deeds.*

smaller subscription school that had been established in Method between 1871 and 1873. In 1895, the frame building that had served as the school was moved to another part of the campus and became the boys' dormitory. In 1915, a brick building was constructed with ten classrooms and an auditorium that cost $10,000.

The school educated Blacks in Method and other parts of Wake County from late 1916 to the early twentieth century. From 1921 to 1922, $1,000 was given from the Rosenwald Foundation to build a teacher's house. By 1923, the school was the first rural school for Blacks that was accredited by the State of North Carolina for teaching the high school academic curriculum.

O'Kelly attended the Tuskegee Conference to learn about trends in progressive education for Blacks. It was at this conference that he met Julius Rosenwald, a businessman and philanthropist whose extraordinary generosity helped to build over five thousand schools and teachers' homes, primarily for Blacks in the rural South. In order for the Berry O'Kelly Training School to receive state accreditation, they needed extra buildings to be built. Financing was secured from Julius Rosenwald. O'Kelly donated ten acres of land, while the Rosenwald Foundation contributed the money.

As part of the building program, a girls' dorm with a dining facility for all the students and faculty was built in 1922. The general classroom building was constructed in 1923. The vocational building, constructed in 1926, was fully equipped with shops, including vocational agricultural labs, room for home economics and a poultry incubation room in the basement. This was called the Agriculture Building. (It is still in service as part of the Method Community Center and is called the Pioneer Building.) By 1927, the complex had eight buildings. In April 1928, a great celebration occurred as the classroom building at the Berry O'Kelly Training School was the 4,000[th] building that the Rosenwald Foundation had helped construct.

The Berry O'Kelly Training School attracted students from all over the state. This four-year high school was the largest high school for Blacks in the state of North Carolina by the year 1931. It trained students in traditional academic and vocational trades. The faculty was small, with three female teachers. Fifteen units of academics were required for graduation.

Additional schools for Black students that were built in the county and across the state caused a decline in boarders and thus a decline in finances. The high school program ended in 1955. Eventually, the elementary school became part of the Wake County school system. The elementary school closed in 1967 as a result of the 1964 Supreme Court ruling outlawing racial segregation in educational systems.

BERRY O'KELLY

Berry O'Kelly was born in Wake County. His mother died in childbirth, and his family members raised him in what was then the Mason Village community. He was named Berry after his mother's uncle. The first job he had with wages was as a houseman for a white family. He had no extra funds to pay for education, so he had very little schooling after attending public school in Chapel Hill. At age twenty-two, he worked in the store owned by C.H. Wood. He earned twelve dollars a month as a salesclerk. With a one-hundred-dollar investment, he eventually became co-partner with Woods in the store. The store was renamed C.H. Woods and Berry O'Kelly store. Woods moved to Oklahoma, and Berry O'Kelly purchased his share and became the sole proprietor of the store.

After purchasing the store, the amount of merchandise that was sold increased. He began to stock shoes, men's work clothes, yard goods and notions. The store served the entire Method community, including Blacks and whites. Eventually, the store met the sanitary code and was able to sell

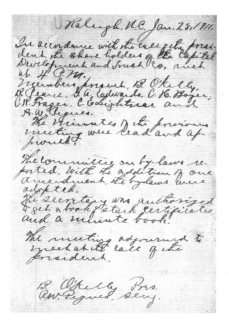

Capital Development and Trust Company meeting minutes, with Berry O'Kelly as president. *Permission of Pettiford family.*

fresh meat, including pork, lamb, roast and steak, as well as oysters when they were in season. John Coggins was allowed to set up a booth beside the store to sell fish on the weekends.

Berry O'Kelly commissioned merchandise sales to area stores and colleges. Because Method was adjacent to the Seaboard Southern Railroad tracks, he built a warehouse to unload fertilizer, farm equipment and other nonperishable goods from the train stop that he was then able to sell. The warehouse and shipping complex supplied foodstuff and merchandise to most of the Raleigh schools and businesses, as well as the surrounding areas. This proximity to the railroad allowed for train service and postal service to the neighborhood. In 1890, a post office was opened at his store, and he became the postmaster. It was a lifetime appointment.

Berry O'Kelly was prominent in Raleigh financial affairs. For many years, he was Raleigh's only commissioned merchant. He was a well-known investor in downtown properties and businesses. His help was requested in setting up Mechanics and Farmers Bank in Raleigh in 1923. He served as vice president and president of that bank. The public's confidence in him was one of the reasons why Mechanics and Farmers Bank was one of only two banks to survive through the Depression in this area. He was president of a shoe company (Raleigh Shoe Company with John T. Turner) and chair of Eagle Life Insurance Company. He was also an investor in the *Raleigh Independent*, an African American newspaper, with Dr. J.W. Love and Charles Keith. He was president of Acme Realty Company and jointly owned a building at 134½ South Wilmington Street with a group of investors called the Capital Development and Trust Company. He was also a founder of People's Investment Company.

He is most well known in Raleigh for consolidating, in 1914, three rural Black schools into the Berry O'Kelly Training School. The vocational training school eventually had an academic component and became the first Black accredited high school in the state of North Carolina. He was also a founding member of the National Negro Business League with Booker T. Washington.

A little-known fact is how influential O'Kelly was in obtaining the 1911 construction of the Western Wake Highway that connected Raleigh to Cary. He was also a trustee at Kittrell College in Kittrell, North Carolina, and a member of the executive committee of the State Interracial Commission. Berry O'Kelly was married to Channie Ligon, and they had no children.

JOHN WILLIAM LIGON

John Ligon's parents were Washington and Amanda Dunn Ligon. He was born on November 12, 1869, in Method, North Carolina. He attended Shaw University, where he graduated in 1889. He also received a theology degree in Chicago. He was pastor of Tupper Memorial Baptist Church in

The John W. Ligon family home (circa 1920s), 573 East Lenoir Street across from Crosby Garfield School. *Author photo.*

1901. He was married to Daisy Jones from Charlotte, North Carolina. He believed strongly in the virtue of education and read to his children every night. When each child was born, he bought them a book on Negroes or authored by a Negro so that they would always be able to learn about their own race and heritage.

John Ligon was principal of Crosby-Garfield School from 1901 to 1919. After becoming principal, he bought a man's house at 573 East Lenoir Street because it was in a red-light district, and he continually complained about the character of the men and women near the school grounds. As his complaints seemed to fall on deaf ears, the gentleman who owned the house taunted him and suggested that he purchase the house himself. So Ligon bought it on a dare!

He ran for city commissioner in 1919 and was subsequently let go from his job because he ran for public office. He said, "I dared to be a man." After leaving the field of education, he continued to preach and also edited a weekly Baptist newspaper called the *Union Reformer*.

LINCOLNVILLE

L incolnville was one of the principal freedmen's villages. It was originally one and one-half miles west of Raleigh on Chapel Hill Road. The village extended to Trinity Road near where the Carter-Finley Stadium sits today. It was set on or near the land of William R. Crawford, who was a Raleigh farmer and meat supplier. Nicknames for the area were "Cooks Hill" and "Beef Hill."

Lincolnville thrived through the end of the nineteenth century. In 1873, changes occurred when the North Carolina Agricultural Association made the decision to relocate the fairgrounds out of East Raleigh. At that point, the area was surrounded and swallowed by the North Carolina Agricultural and Mechanical College (North Carolina State University). In 1904, the area of Lincolnville was obliterated for the construction of the agricultural building that is part of the State Fairgrounds.

Because the community was built around the church of the same name, when the church had to move because of the expansion, the members of the community did the same. After the church was moved to Nowell Road, other families began to move to that area because it was only a few miles from the original Lincolnville site. When the church and community moved to Nowell Road, they became part of the Asbury community. Asbury was located between Raleigh and Cary and was the site of a train stop.

As late as 1980, the area had a store and a dozen homes with approximately fifty inhabitants. Much of the community was still on well water at that time. There was no sewer system, and houses were in much disrepair. Wake County requested, through the state, a grant from the federal government.

Lincolnville aerial photo. *State Archives of North Carolina.*

Two years after the request was made, the grant was received, and the county was able to assist the members of the community in repairing and rebuilding those homes that were in desperate condition. The community flooded often because it was in a low-lying area.

LINCOLNVILLE AME CHURCH

This community was built around a church called Lincolnville AME, which was begun in 1869 as Ephesus Baptist Church. The membership at Ephesus numbered thirty-nine people. Of that number, three colored members were

NORTH CAROLINA,
Wake county.

The foregoing certificate of Sara Weinstein, a notary public of Wake county,
State of North Carolina, is adjudged to be correct. Let the instrument, with the certificate, be registered.

Witness my hand this the 3rd day of March, 1932.

A. C. JONES, Deputy Clerk Superior Court,

Filed for registration at 10.15 A. M. Mar. 3, 1932, and recorded in office of Register of Deeds for Wake county in book 624, page 540, March 9, 1932.

HUNTER ELLINGTON, Register of Deeds,

By_____Deputy.

—————————————————

:::
::   "D E E D."   ::
:: TRUSTEES LINCOLNVILLE M.E. CHURCH,   ::
::   TO   ::
::   STATE'S PRISON.   ::
:::

NORTH CAROLINA, Wake county.

THIS DEED, MAde this the
28 day of January, 1932, by and between Henry Brown, DAvid Blount, John
Blount, A. F. Brown, Moses Jones,
Walter Cain and James Cain, Trustees
of Lincolnville Methodist Episcopal
Church of the County and state aforesaid, parties of the first part to
the State's Prison, a governmental
agency of the State of North Carolina,
party of the second part,

WITNESSETH: That the said
parties of the first part have in consideration of the sum of $1.00 to them in
hand paid, the receipt whereof is hereby duly acknowledged, have given, granted,
bargained, sold and convey unto the said party of the second part, its successors
and assigns forever, all that certain lot or parcel of land lying and being in
Houses Creek Township, Wake county, North Carolina, adjoining the lands now owned
by the State's Prison, containing one quarter of an acre, and more fully described
and defined in a certain deed of conveyame from Tilla Thompson to David Blount
and others by deed bearing date of April 18, 1874, and duly recorded in registry
in Wake county, North Carolina, in book #58, page 577.

TO HAVE AND TO HOLD the same to the use and behoof of the said party of the
second part, its successors and assigns.

And the said parties of the first part covenant to and with the said party
of the second part, its heirs and assigns, that they are the owners of said lot
and have the right to convey the same in fee simple; that the same is free and
clear from any and all encumbrances whatsoever, and that they will forever warrent
and defend the title thereto against the lawful claims of all persons whomsoever.

IN TESTIMONY WHEREOF, said parties of the first part being thereunto duly
licensed and authorized by proper resolution of the Lincolnville Methodist Episcopal
Church have hereunto set their hands and affixed their several seals, the day and
date first above written.

HENRY BROWN,   (SEAL)   A. F. BROWN,   (SEAL)
DANIEL BLOUNT,   (SEAL)   MOSES L. JONES,   (SEAL)
JOHN BLOUNT,   (SEAL)   WALTER CAIN,   (SEAL)
                               JAMES CAIN,   (SEAL)

Above and opposite: A record of the Lincolnville AME Church original land sale for North
Carolina Correctional Center, which became part of North Carolina State University.
Wake County Register of Deeds.

NORTH CAROLINA.
Wake County.

I, A. T. White, as notary public in and for the county and state aforesaid, do hereby certify that this day personally appeared before me Henry Brown, David Blount, John Blount, A. F. Brown, Moses Jones, Walter Kane and James Kane, each of whom acknowledged the due execution of the foregoing deed of conveyance for the intents and purposes therein expressed.

Witness my hand and notarial seal.

(NOTARIAL SEAL)   A. T. WHITE, Notary Public.

My com. exp. February 23, 1933.

NORTH CAROLINA,
Wake county.

The foregoing certificate of A. T. White, a notary public of Wake county, state of North Carolina, is adjudged to be correct. Let the instrument, with the certificates, be registered. Witness my hand this the 3rd day of March, 1932.

A. C. JONES, Deputy Clerk Superior Court.

Filed for registration at 10.20 A. M. March 3, 1932, and recorded in office of Register of Deeds for Wake county in book 624, page 542, March 9, 1932.

HUNTER ELLINGTON, Register of Deeds.

By .... Deputy.

```
:::::::::::::::::::::::::::::::::::::::
::                                 ::
::            "D E E D."           ::
::      VICTORIA PAGE & HUSBAND,   ::
::              TO                 ::
::         THE STATES PRISON.      ::
::                                 ::
:::::::::::::::::::::::::::::::::::::::
```

NORTH CAROLINA, Wake county.

THIS DEED, Made this the 3rd day of March, A. D. 1932, by Victoria Page and Ernest Page, her husband, of the county and state aforesaid, parties of the first part, and The State's Prison, a governmental agency of the State of North Carolina, party of the second part,

WITNESSETH: That the said parties of the first part, for and in consideration of the sum of One dollar, and other good and sufficient considerations, to them moving, the receipt whereof is hereby duly acknowledged, have given, granted, bargained, and sold and conveyed and by these presents, do hereby give, grant, bargain, sell and convey unto the said party of the second part, its successors and assigns, that certain lot or parcel of land lying and being in House Creek Township, Wake county, North Carolina, adjoining and surrounded by other lands belonging to the party of the second part, containing ¼ of an acre, more or less and fully described and defined by a certain map or plot made by R. G. Ball, Engineer, of Raleigh, N.C., which said map or plot has been duly registered and reference thereto is hereby made for detailed description.

TO HAVE AND TO HOLD the same to the use and behoof of the said party of the second part its successors and assigns forever.

And the said parties of the first part covenant to and with the said party of the second part, its successors and assigns that they are the owners of said lands and premises in fee and have a right to convey the same in fee simple; that the same are free and clear from any and all encumbrance, and that they will warrant and defend the title thereto against the lawful claims of all persons whomsoever.

IN TESTIMONY WHEREOF, the said Victoria Page and Ernest Page, her husband, parties of the first part, have hereunto set their hands and affixed, their seals, the day and date first above written.

VICTORIA PAGE,   (SEAL)
ERNEST PAGE,   (SEAL)

listed. The colored membership remained on the church rolls until 1873. There are no names listed in the Ephesus Church history, but it is believed that those three colored people left to organize Lincolnville AME Church between 1872 and 1874.

The Lincolnville AME Church's first building was originally located on or near Trinity Road near the Carter-Finley Stadium. The old cemetery was behind the stadium and was moved in 2012 to the church building that is now on Chapel Hill Road. North Carolina State's expansion and building of the stadium meant that the church was forced to find a different location. According to Katie Jones in an interview in *Culture Town*, "We didn't have any place to build a church, so we tore the church down in the mid-twenties and they hauled the boards down in the woods to somebody's property. The lumber stayed down there until the termites had eaten it up." The land that was donated for the new church site was donated by a church member, Sarah Carrington.

Two of Lincolnville AME's pastors who assisted in building the church were Reverend William D. Cooke and Reverend Patrick James Jordan. Reverend Cooke was born in Warrenton, North Carolina, in February 1860. He was one of eight children and attended Shaw Institute, Howard and Wilberforce College. In 1880, he built Lincolnville AME Church, which cost $700. He also served at Mother Bethel Church in Philadelphia. Reverend Jordan was born in 1862 near Wilmington. He spent some time attending Shaw Institute but was considered a self-made man in terms of his education. He received a doctorate of divinity from Kittrell College. While he served at Lincolnville, the church was built at a cost of $350.

The Lincolnville trustees purchased the original 1868 one-room wooden church building from Ephesus Baptist Church in 1927. It was located across the street, north of the railroad tracks from where that building is today (6767 Hillsborough Street). They took it apart and hauled it by wagon to the new location that was at 900 Nowell Road. The lumber was reassembled to make it look like the original building. The $127 cost of the building was paid to Ephesus Church members in fifty-cent pieces, quarters, dimes, nickels and pennies. The money was carried to the Ephesus Church by Brother Moses Jones.

Brother Jones had trouble moving the church building. The original windowsills were too long to carry in his wagon. They were fifty to fifty-five feet long. He uncoupled his wagon and made an extension out of two-by-fours, so he was able to take all the sills without cutting them.

The pews, which were donated in 1939, were also too big to move. The members from Ephesus agreed to cut them to fit the wagon extension at a cost of five dollars per pew. The church members from Lincolnville were taxed to pay to have the pews cut. Women were taxed fifty cents and men taxed one dollar in order to pay the cost of the pew cutting.

Other materials from the church were salvaged, including an old church bell. The church bell originally hung in a tree in the yard and then was placed in the steeple. According to the Lincolnville historian, it was the custom for the first person who arrived to go into the belfry, take hold of the dangling rope and pull the bell as a signal to the community that it was time for the church service. The church also had a pot-bellied stove, upright piano, tambourine collection, communion rail, carpet, broad pine bark pulpit and the oil lamps from the original church.

The historical church building was eventually purchased by the State of North Carolina and now sits in the Village of Yesteryear at the North Carolina State Fairgrounds. After that sale, Lincolnville AME Church purchased land at 6400 Chapel Hill Road, where it is now located.

BROOKLYN

The location of the neighborhood named Brooklyn was the crossroads one mile northwest of Raleigh, close to or adjacent to Devereaux Farms. That can be found on the 1881 Shaffer map of Raleigh. Brooklyn was considered in the same direction as Oberlin Village, although it was in the northwest part of the city.

There were two churches in the neighborhood in 1877. One was a small white Methodist congregation. In 1893, St. Augustine's Episcopal Church started. Many of the "upper crust" Blacks who were at St. Augustine's Institute were members. By 1899, St. Augustine's Episcopal Church had moved.

The neighborhood was mixed with residents of both Black and white races. Over a period of time, there was an encroachment of the white population. As late as 1905, Blacks still lived there, but the white community developed around them. When Brooklyn first started, there were about one hundred residents in the neighborhood. The houses were made almost entirely of wood, but there could be a little stone or brick in their construction.

CANNON LANDS/HAYTI/MANLY'S HOMESTEAD

CANNON LANDS

Cannon Lands was located in southwest Raleigh. It was in the center of the Cannon family land west of the North Carolina Railroad tracks. After the Civil War, the estate of Robert Cannon was subdivided into small parcels and mostly sold to freedmen.

The parcels were also sold to white speculators who built housing for Blacks. There were fifty or more one-story wooden houses in the 1870s, like many of the houses for Blacks that were built across the city. The northern section of the land that was bounded by South Street, the railroad tracks, West Street and Cannon Street became a Black residential neighborhood. By 1872, forty homes had been built in the neighborhood. By 1882, an additional ten homes had been built. The occupations of those living in Cannon Lands included teachers, carpenters, laborers, farmers, brick masons and a Western Union messenger.

HAYTI

Hayti was former plantation land that was below South Street and ran southeast along the railroad tracks across from Cannon Lands. The area was known as Hayti for at least twenty years and made up most of what was later known as Fourth Ward and eventually became known as Southside. In the

1960s, this entire area was destroyed by the city as part of urban renewal to build what is now Martin Luther King Boulevard and the downtown portion of the McDowell-Salisbury Connector.

In 1866, the six acres of land was subdivided. The land formed a triangle that was south of the North Carolina Railroad tracks, east to Manly Street and north of South Street, straddling Fayetteville Road. The subdivision consisted of small lots that were available to newly freed Blacks for a minimum down payment. Nine Black families purchased land there. Within weeks, three of the families had started to build houses.

Blacks and whites purchased the property in this area. The deeds described "the new part of the City of Raleigh, south of the railroad, known as 'Hayti,' included the old Street, which is about to be re-opened" behind the palace (old Governor's Mansion, which is the Memorial Auditorium).

The Raleigh Cooperative Land and Building Association helped William Scott and his wife purchase a lot in Hayti in 1870. John R. Caswell, a Black Wake County commissioner and grocer, purchased a home there in 1870. By 1872, approximately two dozen structures had been built. The name Hayti first appeared in print in the 1875 city directory. The occupations of many of the residents included laborer, carpenter, waiter and hostler. (A hostler is someone who looks after the horses at an inn or is a groom or stableman.)

Amos Solomon was a white resident who lived in the neighborhood. He and other whites were characterized as poor. In many cases, the neighborhoods in the Black sections were characterized as poor first and Black second. However, whites could generally move out into other neighborhoods, while Blacks were not allowed in white neighborhoods due to the law. Reverend Fisk Brewer purchased land for Washington Graded School for the freedmen here.

MANLY'S HOMESTEAD

Governor Manly's mansion and grounds had blocked the southern end of Fayetteville Street since 1815. The land was bordered by the Daniel Barringer mansion on one side. The farm of Moses Bledsoe took up the land that was south of the Barringer estate and went past the city limits. Up until 1865, that land was uninhabited.

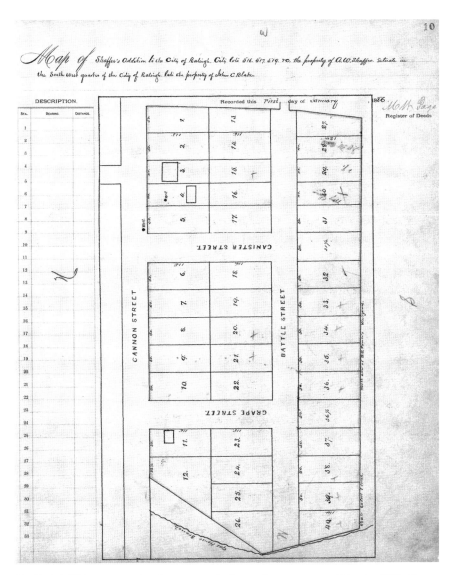

Shaffer's Addition map to the city property in the southwest quarter of the city. *Wake County Register of Deeds.*

The purchase of the Barringer estate in 1870 for the permanent home of the Raleigh Institute (which became Shaw University) is one reason that caused further development of South Raleigh into a Black residential area. The other reason was the establishment of the freedmen's school (which became Washington School) on South Street near the Manly home.

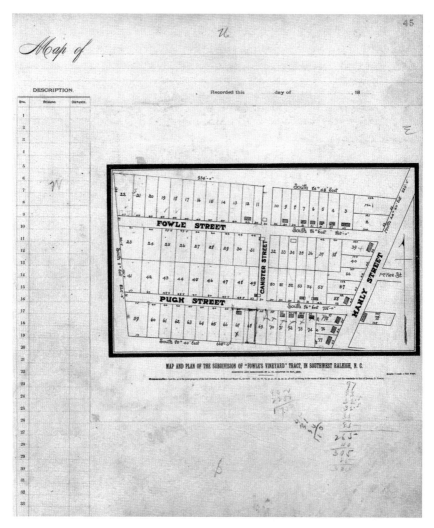

Fowles Vineyard, Manly Street adjacent to the present site of Washington School. The area called Fourth Ward was destroyed during urban renewal between 1967 and 1970. *Wake County Register of Deeds.*

Once the heirs made the decision to sell the land, a triangle-shaped block was created across the North Carolina Railroad tracks from Hayti. The area was south of Governor Manly's mansion. It was divided by Lookout Street, which became Worth Street. Eventually, it was divided into thirty-four odd-shaped plots. Sales of the area began in 1873.

One of Governor Manly's former slaves purchased the dwelling and lot where they had lived during slavery. In 1873, B.H. Dunston, a Black Raleigh police officer, purchased a home. By 1881, eighteen additional houses had been built. The area characterized as Shaffer's Addition was a five-acre tract of land purchased by a developer, A.W. Shaffer, in 1886. He divided the five acres into forty lots. The area that was a vineyard between Shaffer's land and the city's southern boundary was owned by a man named Fowle. He built a small row of cottages that fronted on Manly Street. There were eventually seventy-seven lots in that track by the year 1899. All of these areas began to merge and created a segregated Black residential district.

Macedonia New Life Church

Watts Chapel was an integrated congregation in 1860 that disbanded. The Black members began meeting at the close of the Civil War (1867) and organized in 1878. The church met in Baptist Grove on the site that was also known as Moore Square. In March 1870, the General Assembly authorized the move of that building used by the Baptists to a lot west of the Governor's Palace (site of Memorial Auditorium) "to be used as a house of worship by the colored people of Raleigh known as Christians."

They were forced to move to the Jenkins plot of land near the Fayetteville Street crossing and later to the Manly Street space. They became known as Manly Street Christian Church, then Manly Street United Church of Christ, and their location was in Fourth Ward.

In the 1970s, after the Raleigh City Urban Renewal and Planning Commission plans forced them to move, they relocated to Rock Quarry Road. The name was changed to Laodicea United Christian Church. They are now known as Macedonia New Life Church and remain at the Rock Quarry Road location.

First Cosmopolitan Church

In 1895, the Fayetteville Street Little Mission Church was housed at 751 Fayetteville Street after the land was purchased from the Little Mission Church for a group of sixteen members. The church was eventually renamed Fayetteville Street Baptist Church. In 1969, it was renamed First Cosmopolitan Baptist Church because of its relocation due to the decision made by the Raleigh City Urban Renewal and Planning Commission. The church now sits on Cross Link Road in the back of the Lyndhurst Manor neighborhood.

FIRST CONGREGATIONAL CHURCH

First Congregational Church was originally established by the American Missionary Association (AMA) in a one-room wooden building serving as the Freedmen's School on the corner of Manly and South Streets. Reverend Fisk P. Brewer was the leader of the school. This establishment led to the beginning of Washington Graded School for colored people, which had seven grades.

Reverend J.J. Mott was the first pastor of First Congregational, which was located in Raleigh's Fourth Ward. The first Black pastor was Reverend

Boy Scout Troop 52 on Fayetteville Street in front of Sir Walter Hotel. This photo includes Richard E. Wimberley Jr., Wake County's first Black Eagle Scout. *Wimberley family photo.*

First Congregational Church, corner of Manly and South Streets. It is a frame building with a corner tower erected circa 1896 in Manly's Homestead area. *The Albert Barden Collection, State Archives of North Carolina.*

George Smith, who came in 1877. The ownership of the building was transferred from the AMA to the City of Raleigh in 1882, and the church was incorporated fifteen years later in 1907.

Reverend Perfect R. DeBerry, pastor as of 1909, started many youth activities. These included:

- The first chartered Boy Scout troop for Negroes in the state;
- The first city nursery school; and
- The first city trade school.

As of 1918, the church became independent of the AMA. In the 1950s, under Reverend Howard Cunningham, the church worked on improving race relations by holding joint services and activities with Community United Church of Christ, Davie Street Presbyterian Church and Pullen Memorial Baptist Church.

In 1976, due to the decision made by the Raleigh City Urban Renewal and Planning Commission, the building was torn down after the church was forced to move from the original location. The congregation has been in its present site—on Creech Road near Southeast Raleigh High School—since July 1977.

HUNGRY NECK

Hungry Neck is in a low-lying area east of East Street at the foot of Edenton Street. The community was developed north of the Old Fairgrounds. Today, it includes the streets from New Bern Avenue to Jones Street to North Swain Street.

The land was sold by the Raleigh Cooperative Land and Building Group. The 1872 map shows a collection of twenty or more tiny houses on the fringe of the city. Hungry Neck was separated from other Black neighborhoods by New Bern Avenue. The white middle-class populations lived to the west of the Hungry Neck area. The community was home to blue-collar workers including carpenters, bricklayers, laborers and draymen.

One of the homes still standing on East Edenton Street was purchased by Amos Brooks, who paid $7 down in 1879. He is believed to have been a freed slave who worked in a livery stable. The wood frame house cost $300 and was paid off at $5 a month. At his death, his will not only left the home

> ——The eastern end of Newbern avenue, poetically designated as "Hungry Neck, needs the attention of the city authorities. The refuse, etc., thrown into back alleys, and the stagnant pools in its vicinity is well calculated to infest the community with some malignant disease.

Conditions in Hungry Neck neighborhood. *From the* Raleigh News, *August 14, 1879.*

to his widow and ten children, but he also left two new feather beds, two small tables and a large dining table.

In 1875, the Democrats gerrymandered the area to make it become part of the Second Ward in the city of Raleigh. In 1881, the streets were laid out between the rows of one-room frame cottages. Before 1891, Edenton Street continued beyond Swain Street up into the Idlewild area.

One of the citizens who lived in the area was named Oliver Rhone. He managed the Union Hall Billiard and Saloon establishment. Cox Memorial Church was started in this area in 1887 with twenty-five members.

Neville's Episcopal Church

Little is known about this church, but it may have been organized in the 1860s in J.P. Neville's meetinghouse in southeast Raleigh between Cabarrus and East Lenoir Streets near what was later named Swain Street. The exclusively white YMCA bought the building prior to the war, and it was used to teach poor children in.

ST. PETERSBURG

The neighborhood called St. Petersburg was east of East Street at the foot of Martin Street. It actually runs from Hargett Street to Camden Street to Davie Street to East Street. St. Petersburg was near the Old Fairgrounds site. Martin Street extended through St. Petersburg by the year 1872.

We are not able to find where the name came from. St. Petersburg was a division of the land owned by Governor Charles Manly. The land was rapidly sold off during the early years of Reconstruction to Black individuals and entrepreneurs. The parcels that were sold were different sizes. This was one of the most racially mixed residential districts in the city of Raleigh during Reconstruction. The economic conditions of the Blacks and the whites were very much alike; they were blue-collar workers.

According to records, white people did not move into the area after the 1870s. Those whites who lived in the community remained and didn't move out. By 1900, the area was all Black. The white-owned properties were all rented to Black families. In 1873, the name St. Petersburg disappeared from the deed book. In 1875, the deed book listed Martin Street. In 1881, there were twenty-four houses on Martin Street past East Street.

COTTON PLACE/IDLEWILD

J ohn W. Cotton owned a fourteen-acre plantation that he called Idlewild. After his death, the estate was sold to the North Carolina Land Company and subdivided between 1860 and 1900. New Bern Avenue divided the plantation's land into two separate freedmen's villages: Idlewild and Cotton Place.

COTTON PLACE

Cotton Place was located on the south side of New Bern Avenue. Its boundaries extended from Hargett Street, just opposite the Old Fairgrounds, east of the city boundary, to New Bern Avenue. Cotton Place separated the antebellum mansion of Idlewild Plantation from the housing development of freedmen.

The land that was purchased was subdivided into fifty lots. Some of those lots were purchased by the Raleigh Cooperative Land Association. In 1872, twenty homes were constructed on the block. By 1880, thirty homes had been constructed. The homes that were built were generally two-room frame dwellings. Between 1899 and 1900, the city directories show a high number of Blacks living in the area. One of the people who lived in the neighborhood was Charles N. Hunter, an educator and principal at Crosby and Oberlin Schools.

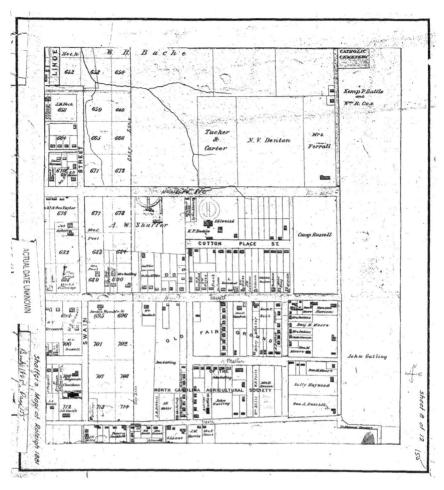

Idlewild Plantation between New Bern Avenue and Cotton Place; Camp Russell (became Confederate Old Soldiers' Home). It had small lots for rental housing. The original State Fairgrounds are near the bottom. *Wake County Register of Deeds.*

IDLEWILD

Idlewild was to the north of New Bern Avenue. Its boundaries were New Bern Avenue to the south, Oakwood Avenue to the north, Tarboro Road to the east and Linden Street to the west.

As with Shaw University, the Idlewild community grew up around St. Augustine's College. Many of the people who lived in Idlewild were originally former slaves or were part of the first generation of people who were born

This Idlewild stone marker denotes history as part of the city's Edenton New Bern History Walk, developed by North Central Community Advisory Council. *City of Raleigh.*

free. The first residents had goals that they wanted to achieve, including owning their own homes and educating their children.

In a *News and Observer* interview, Ella Clark stated that people took what jobs they could and pinched their pennies. "People had to save money to buy bootstraps before they could pull themselves up." There was a broad mix of residents, including laborers, teachers and doctors who worked at St. Agnes Hospital. There were also washerwomen, yardmen and domestics for the white families who lived in nearby Oakwood.

Howard Pullen, interviewed for the book *Culture Town*, said that neighbors helped neighbors in the community. As a child growing up in the neighborhood, he would watch baseball games at the old ballpark off New Bern Avenue. He said the seats were reserved for whites and there was only a small section for Blacks to sit in, but the tickets were expensive. They carved holes in the fence so they could watch the games. Pullen and his family lived in a white house at the corner of North State and Lane Streets that had been owned by Dr. Lemuel Delany, a doctor at St. Agnes Hospital and brother of Sadie and Bessie Delany.

St. Augustine's opened a training center, Bishop Tuttle Memorial Training School, that eventually became a neighborhood recreation center known as Tuttle Center. It is on Tarboro Road. Community workshops, meetings and dances were held there. It was also a daycare center in the 1950s and 1960s. (More details on Tuttle Center can be found under St. Augustine's College.)

The residents of the Idlewild community received good benefits because of their proximity to the college. The college provided help with healthcare, Sunday school, kindergarten and a clothing store. There was also a missionary guild and a women's group that counseled on childcare and nutrition.

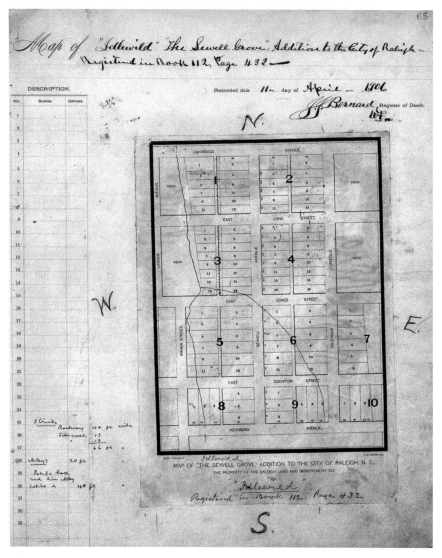

Above: "Sewell Grove" was added to Idlewild subdivision by Raleigh Land and Improvement Co. The lots were intended for whites, but few sold. The land was eventually sold to Black customers. *Wake County Register of Deeds.*

Opposite: The 1893 Idlewild addition where O'Rorke and Maple Avenue were renamed Hicks Street. This map shows the alleys behind lots where trash and sewage were placed for pickup. *Wake County Register of Deeds.*

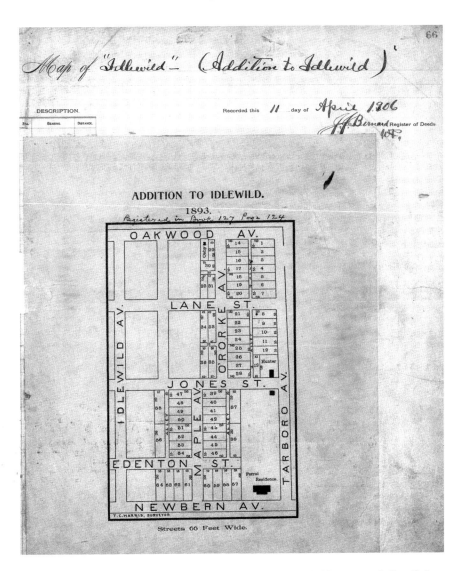

Mildred James, also interviewed by the *News and Observer* and for *Culture Town*, lived at 310 Heck Street all her life. This was a two-story wooden frame house that her father purchased in 1910. She belonged to First Baptist Church. She remembered that when the family moved into the house, there was a cotton patch and a sweet potato patch across the street. Her family owned a cow named Mary, and her mother would sell the cow's milk to people in the neighborhood. Her father worked for the Seaboard Railroad, which was considered one of the best jobs in the community for Black men. He left the company after having an argument with a supervisor who called him a boy.

ST. AUGUSTINE'S COLLEGE/ST. AGNES HOSPITAL/ BISHOP TUTTLE MEMORIAL TRAINING SCHOOL

St. Augustine's College was chartered on July 19, 1867. The school had four students when it opened on January 13, 1868. It opened in the Howard School House, which was in the Union barracks at Camp Russell on the Old Fairgrounds property. The camp was originally called Camp Ellis. It was named for North Carolina Confederate governor John W. Ellis.

The Freedmen's Commission of the Protestant Episcopal Church and the North Carolina leaders of the Protestant Episcopal Church decided in 1865 to open a school "for the purpose of educating teachers for the colored people of the State of North Carolina." They also wanted to prepare Negro men for the Episcopalian ministry. Reverend J. Brinton Smith headed the Educational Commission but had been operating an industrial school for children of the poor. The commission felt the education of former slaves was important and there was a need for Negro teachers. It was determined that the commission would locate teachers who were willing to travel to the South. They would raise funds to pay them and get the diocese to accept them. The southern dioceses were determined to cooperate.

Reverend Smith resigned from the commission to take the post. He became the first principal and was one of the first incorporators for the school, which was called St. Augustine's Normal School and Collegiate Institute. The other incorporators included Reverend Richard S. Mason, rector of Christ Church; Reverend Albert Smedes, founder of St. Mary's College; and other directors from Episcopal churches in the area. They also included General William Cox and Dr. Kemp P. Battle.

The school was named for St. Augustine, Bishop of Hippo. He was born at Tagaste, Africa, in AD 354. His mother was a Christian, and his father was a pagan. They sent him to Carthage to complete his education, but he devoted himself to pleasure. St. Ambrose, Bishop of Milan, converted him, and upon reading Paul's epistles, Augustine changed his life and his character. He became assistant to the Bishop of Hippo, and in AD 395, he became the Bishop of Hippo. His full name was Aurelius Augustinus.

In 1867, Reverend Smith received $25,000 from the estate of Reverend Charles Avery of Pittsburgh, Pennsylvania, who had left his estate for the education of former slaves. The Freedmen's Bureau gave $6,243 in cash as well as the surplus barracks building that had been used to start the school. The barracks building that had been originally used was moved to the purchased property in order to allow students to move out of Reverend

This St. Augustine's College stone marker also mentions St. Monica's Catholic School, built to educate Black students in 1930. *City of Raleigh.*

Smith's home. The funds received were used to purchase the Seven Springs property where the school is now located. The first building was dedicated on January 16, 1869.

The land for the school was purchased from the Henry Seawell family. It had been the summer home of Willie Jones, who was a Revolutionary War hero and friend of President Thomas Jefferson. Henry Seawell was the state treasurer, a Superior Court judge of law and equity and a Superior Court judge. He was also a member of the North Carolina House of Representatives over a twenty-five-year period. Part of the 110 acres that was purchased for the school was inside the city limits.

Once classes began, in what was then called Howard Hall, there were forty-three students enrolled. Twenty-six of the students were boarders. Reverend Smith wrote, "I see no difference intellectually between them and white children." He did not allow the teachers to take part in any political activities, and there was a "no tuition" policy for the school. The cost of board was eight dollars a month, but not all students were able to pay. Every student had to work. The male students were required to work in

20	ANNUAL CATALOGUE OF

DAILY ROUTINE

6:00 A.M.	Rising Bell
6:25	Inspection
6:35	Breakfast
7:15–8:10	Study Hour
8:1	Morning Prayer
8:30–9:10	First Recitation Period
9:10–9:50	Second Period
9:50–10:30	Third Period
10:30–11:10	Fourth Period
11:10–11:20	Recess
11:20–12:00	Fifth Period
12:00–12:40 P. M.	Sixth Period
12:40–1:15	Seventh Period
1:25	Dinner
2:10–4:10	Industrial Training and Work
4:10–6:10	Recreation
6:15	Evening Prayer
6:50	Supper
7:30–9:00	Study Hour
9:45	Lights Out

FOR INDUSTRIAL STUDENTS

7:15 A. M	Begin Work
1:00 P. M	Stop Work
2:10	Work
3:30	Stop Work
4:00–6:10	Evening School
7:30–9:00	Study Hour

St. Augustine's Normal School and College daily routine (1915). *DigitalNC, State Library of North Carolina.*

the field and gardens that provided the food for students and faculty. They also worked in construction, helping to build the classrooms and dormitories. The girls cooked and did the house cleaning. Those students who were intellectually ahead tutored other students.

At no time was the thought of integrated education entertained. After a four-year stint as principal, Dr. Smith suddenly and mysteriously died. Reverend John Eston Cook Smedes became the acting principal and remained with the school for twelve years.

The second of the first two school buildings was the principal's residence, but it became the girls' dorm. The girls slept in cots in curtained alcoves. The boys slept four to a room in their dorm. All meals were taken together in the Smith building. Each day's class schedule was based on the type of students' activities. For day students, classes ran from 8:15 a.m. to 1:20 p.m.; trade students worked from 7:00 a.m. to 4:20 p.m. on the campus and then attended night school for two to three hours each night.

By 1872, there were 110 students enrolled; 32 of them lived on the campus. During the early 1870s, there were forty acres of campus land. An additional $25,000 was received from the Barry Fund to assist. By the 1890s, the school had a silo and hydraulic ram. At some point, Reverend Smith and the geometry students at the school laid out the sections of Oakwood Cemetery, where he eventually was buried.

On March 6, 1883, a fire destroyed all of the original buildings that had been erected under the work of Reverend Smith except the principal's home and the Smith building. This included the main building, which contained a chapel, library, classrooms and offices. The fire spread to the dining hall, dorms and the small cottage. The Negro city fire company and students helped diligently to put the fire out. The white fire company would not fight

Lyman Building (1886), a four-story brick building that was the site of the chapel, classrooms and men's dormitory. It was named for Episcopal bishop Theodore B. Lyman and demolished in 1960. *State Archives of North Carolina.*

the fires at Negro places throughout the community. The Black company was poorly equipped for the size of the fire.

The cost of the loss of the buildings was between $12,000 and $16,000. Only half of that amount was covered by insurance. All of the masonry and carpentry work that was done at the school was by the students who were in industrial trade classes. The bricks were made on the campus grounds by student labor. The stones in other buildings were brought from a quarry in a grove near the spring that was located on the school grounds. As a result of the fire, the trustees and administration decided that all further buildings would be made of brick. Students quarried stone under Vice Principal Henry Delany's direction and learned how to place the stones from William H. Haywood, Jerry Smith and Washington Hayes, the stonemasons who taught these classes. The assembly hall, chapel, library and Lyman Building were all erected by student labor.

By the end of the Smith administration, students entered the school at the fourth or fifth grade level. Once this was completed, they went on to the prep course and from there to the normal course, which was considered advanced elementary. Following that was an academic or college prep course and then a collegiate course that was comparable to the freshman year of college. Many students would leave after one year, and sometimes after one semester, to begin to teach in Negro schools.

In 1883, the qualifications for admission included the following:

- The ability to read and write
- Knowledge of the fundamental operations of arithmetic

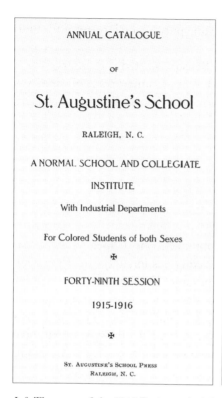

ANNUAL CATALOGUE

OF

St. Augustine's School

RALEIGH, N. C.

A NORMAL SCHOOL AND COLLEGIATE

INSTITUTE

With Industrial Departments

For Colored Students of both Sexes

☩

FORTY-NINTH SESSION

1915-1916

☩

ST. AUGUSTINE'S SCHOOL PRESS
RALEIGH, N. C.

St. Augustine's—
School, RALEIGH, N. C.

Collegiate Department

under graduates of Oberlin, Maryville and Yale Colleges.

Normal and Preparatory Departments

under careful teachers.

TERMS: $7 per month (Incidental Fee $2 per year).
Most students pay **$5 in Cash** and $2 in work.
Students may work their way and go to school at night.
TRAINING SCHOOL FOR NURSES. Board and tuition free.
TRADE SCHOOL. Instruction in building, plastering, cooking and dressmaking. Board and tuition free.

Rev. A. B. HUNTER,
Principal.

Left: The cover of the 1915 St. Augustine's Normal School and College catalogue. *DigitalNC, State Library of North Carolina.*

Right: An advertisement for students wishing to attend St. Augustine's College. *From the Gazette, July 31, 1897.*

- Knowledge of the first lessons of geography
- Preparation sufficient to commence the study of grammar.

Tuition at this point was eight dollars a month unless special arrangements were made to reduce it to five dollars a month. In 1885, the first diplomas were awarded.

In 1888, Reverend Aaron B. Hunter and his wife, Sarah, came to the school. They remained for fifty years. One of Reverend Hunter's desires was to create a trade school something like Hampton Institute. He began to form a bricklaying and masonry class in 1897. There were seven to eight men in each class under a mason so that they could receive practical work in brick and stone construction and plastering and could build the campus structures. Eventually, a print shop was added. They were not only able to print work on campus, but they also took outside jobs. Carpentry, farming, sheet metal and iron works became part of the industrial training program, and that lasted through 1933.

A gift of $1,600 in 1896, from May Benson, started the library, which was subsequently named after her. A 64-acre adjoining tract of land was purchased to complete the 110-acre campus. There was a family atmosphere at the school.

St. Agnes Training School and Hospital

Sarah Hunter had a heart for the community. She helped establish St. Agnes Training School for Nurses by speaking passionately about the need for healthcare for the people in the community. St. Agnes was started for two reasons. The first was to care for the sick people who lived outside the city limits and were not able to go to Rex Hospital. The second reason was to train a "refined class of young women to intelligently care for the sick and enable them to have a profession which would place them in a position to always demand good remuneration and gain a good livelihood in an intelligent manner."

In 1895, Hunter spoke to the women's auxiliary at the Protestant Episcopal Church conference in Minneapolis about the need. Mr. I.R. Collins of Chicago donated $600 to the cause if the hospital would be named in honor of his late wife, Agnes. An anonymous $500 gift followed. The cost of the building was about $30,000. The stone for the building was quarried on the school grounds and placed by the students, who also did the plastering. One of those students was the son of Bishop Henry Delany who would become Dr. Lemuel Delany.

The school was established on October 19, 1896. It began in the former principal's campus house known as Sutton House. Hunter was superintendent from 1896 to 1920. The hospital charged patients $1.50 a week. This included board, nursing and medical attention from doctors. The doctors who were in attendance included Dr. L.A. Scruggs (part of the first graduating class of Shaw's Leonard Medical School), Dr. Kemp Battle, Dr. Augustus Knox, Dr. W.I. Royster, Dr. Richard H. Lewis (who specialized in diseases of the eye, ear, throat and nose), Dr. James McKee (who specialized in diseases of women and children) and Dr. Hubert Royster (who was the chief surgeon as well as dean of the medical department at UNC).

8   ANNUAL CATALOGUE OF

St. Agnes Hospital

Rev. A. B. Hunter, *Principal and Chaplain*
Mrs. A. B. Hunter, *Superintendent and Treasurer*

STAFF

Dr. Hubert A. Royster, *Surgeon-in-Chief*
Dr. Henry G. Turner, *Assistant Surgeon*
Dr. Hubert Haywood, *Physician*
Dr. Aldert S. Root, *Obstetrician and Pediadrist*
Dr. Claude O. Abernethy, *Genito-Urinary
    and Skin Diseases*
Drs. Lewis, Battle and Wright, *Diseases of the
    Eye, Ear, Nose and Throat*
Dr. Jennie A. Duncan, *Resident Physician*
Dr. Lemuel T. Delany, *Assistant*

CONSULTING STAFF

Dr. A. W. Knox, *Surgery*
Dr. W. I. Royster, *Medicine*
Dr. Claude O. Abernethy, *Medicine*
Dr. William Moncure, *Orthopedic Surgery*

ST. AGNES HOSPITAL TRAINING SCHOOL FOR NURSES

Dr. Jennie A. Duncan, *Superintendent of Nurses*
Mrs. Lottie R. Jackson, *Head Nurse*
Dr. Judge B. Davis, *Interne*

INSTRUCTORS

Dr. H. A. Royster
Dr. Jennie A. Duncan
Dr. J. O. Plummer
Dr. J. B. Davis
Mrs. Lottie R. Jackson
Miss Bertha Richards

Left: A list of staff and instructors for St. Agnes Hospital. *DigitalNC, State Library of North Carolina.*

Below: The 1914 graduating class of nurses from St. Agnes Hospital. *DigitalNC, State Library of North Carolina.*

A GRADUATING CLASS OF NURSES

The first surgical operation took place on April 6, 1897. The building was eventually able to accommodate seventy-five to one hundred patients. It was one of the largest hospitals for colored people in the country. Upon opening, the building had accommodations for the resident physician, the head nurse, twenty-three patients and sixteen student nurses. The hospital was a charitable one.

When the school first opened, student nurses could receive a diploma in eighteen months. They were then able to earn fifteen to twenty dollars a week in private duty nursing. The first female resident physician was Dr. Catherine P. Hayden. She graduated from the University of Colorado in 1894 and served at St. Agnes from 1900 through 1912. She was succeeded by Dr. Jenny A. Duncan, a 1910 graduate from the University of Illinois. The third physician was Dr. Mary D. Glendon, an 1893 Northwestern University women's medicine graduate.

The head nurse at St. Agnes was Marie Burgess, a Black woman. She was also the matron. There were three other nurses on staff with her. They all lived in the attic of the building. The hospital was intended mainly for women and children, but the first patient was a man with typhoid fever.

The original building that St. Agnes was situated in did not have ideal conditions. Mary Lewis Wyche, who was the supervisor of Rex Hospital training school for nurses in 1894, said, "There was no plumbing facilities, no screens, no electric lights, no gas for cooking or lighting—only oil lamps. For laundry equipment three ordinary tubs served, together with a big iron pot in the yard for boiling clothes, and a flat iron heater. The office was reception room, doctor's living room, dining room, surgeon's dressing room on operating days, and sometimes the morgue." Further description states that there was one faucet in the kitchen, and water was supplemented by that from the nearby spring. The spring water was cooler than what came out of the faucet. The water had to be heated on the wood stove, which was the only source of heat for the building.

In 1908, the original structure was a four-story stone building with a seventy-five-bed capacity. In 1922, during fundraising activities, three white-robed members of the Raleigh Ku Klux Klan walked into the meeting and donated five ten-dollar bills as the first payment of a one-hundred-dollar contribution to the hospital.

Dear Sir:
Believing in the sincerity of the movement and being in sympathy with the furthering of such a worthy and beneficent cause, the Klan hereby declares

its interest in the success and future welfare of the St. Agnes Hospital for colored people and hereby makes known its desire and willingness to lend support.

It gives great pleasure, therefore, at this opportunity to tender, as a visible sign, the pledge of the Raleigh Klan to this cause, written for the sum of one hundred dollars. And enclosed herewith are five ten-dollar bills as the first payment on this pledge.

With the hopes of the Klan for the great success of the campaign.
Yours very truly,
Kligrapp
Raleigh Klan No. 1, Realm of North Carolina

Prior to the founding of St. Agnes, the 1868 North Carolina Constitution required care of the poor, the unfortunate and orphans. Churches and women's groups opened facilities for those with health issues. St. John's Guild was one of those and was organized in 1877 with a library and hospital. It was started by Reverend Edward Robbins Rick, rector of Church of the

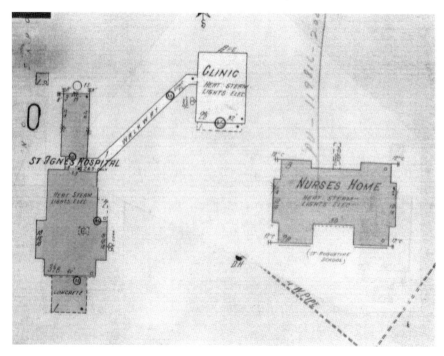

The 1938 Sanborn Fire Map for St. Agnes Hospital, Clinic and Nurses' Home. *North Carolina Maps, State Archives of North Carolina.*

Good Shepherd. The hospital opened in 1878 in a house on Wilmington Street but was inside the city limits.

In 1880, four Black men who had been injured in an accident on the railroad tracks were admitted to the hospital, to the consternation of many white Raleigh residents. By 1893, the hospital had closed, and Rex Hospital began operation in 1894. The Klan was no doubt happy to support St. Agnes in order to not have integrated healthcare facilities.

By 1928, St. Agnes had been approved for the instruction of interns. This lasted until 1954. In 1936, St. Agnes had one hundred beds. It also had one dozen local doctors on staff and up to twenty-seven thousand patient days each year. At that time, 75 percent of the work done was charitable. The city and the county could not do without the facility.

During World War II, St. Agnes participated in the government training programs for nurses as contributors to the war effort. This allowed physician training to occur. Residencies in obstetrics, gynecology and surgery were held there. By 1942, the hospital's finances were limited, and the board of trustees at St. Augustine's had deeded the hospital to an independent board to receive public funds for care of indigent persons. "This action was occasioned by ruling of the city council that public money could no longer be given to a private institution." The property reverted to the college when the hospital ceased to operate after the integrated Wake County Medical Center opened in 1960.

THE BISHOP TUTTLE MEMORIAL TRAINING SCHOOL

The Bishop Tuttle Memorial Training School was a national center that was created under the auspices of the Protestant Episcopal Church for the training of Negro men and women for leadership and Christian social service. It was situated on the campus of St. Augustine's College. The school was established in 1925 to train people in social work for both the church and secular fields and offered a two-year course in social work and religious education. In order to matriculate, a student had to have graduated from a four-year school. Although several students completed the program, the school eventually closed. The center's work continued.

In 1931, Reverend and Mrs. Hunter gifted a three-room house for the original center to be housed in. It was for "Negroes in the community…to use leisure time in creative and recreational activities stimulating interest in simple things, spiritual development, skill with the hands, and better health habits, that was preventing juvenile delinquency and training into useful happy citizenship."

In 1933, lots were purchased to the north and east of the house and made into play areas for the community. Funds increased when the United Way began to support the programming, which included a nursery school from 7:30 a.m. to 5:30 p.m. daily; childcare; teen programs for after school; and adult programs. There was a monthly attendance of about five thousand people.

The Bishop Tuttle Center was a Community Chest Agency as well. Community Chest funds were created and financed by private contributions for aiding various charitable organizations and welfare agencies. They were widely used across the country for fundraising before becoming the United Way in the 1950s.

The building hosted the mothers' clubs; provided full library service; and had a restroom for hospital visitors. There were active clubs in the following areas: homemaking, cooking, sewing, gardening, handicrafts, employment service, dancing, preschool education, tennis/sports, adult education, debates, singing and playground supervision. These clubs served between five hundred children and three hundred adults on a regular basis. Although the training school closed in 1940, the activities of the Tuttle Center continued for decades. (In fact, the author attended daycare there.)

One of Sarah Hunter's desires was that the community would be helped by the presence of St. Augustine's College. As part of this community outreach, she organized mothers' meetings. These Friday afternoon gatherings allowed mothers to discuss housekeeping, childcare and other subjects. Most of the time, the attendance was close to one hundred women. One of the projects that was funded through the mothers' meeting was to purchase a small plot of land for a cemetery. A missionary store was also created. Women's auxiliaries and others sent packages of new and used clothing to the center for distribution to the community. Purchases were restricted to members of the mothers' meetings and the students at the college. A small registration fee and admittance card were required in order to purchase items.

A Penny Savings Bank, which was a branch of the Penny Provident Bank of New York City, was also started here. The revenues from the store were used to help with hospital maintenance. They were also used for the addition of a water tank for a supply of spring water for residents who did not have clean water supplies.

Other community activities included the Brotherhood of St. Andrew. This organization conducted religious services on Sundays for tenants at the Fisher Farm, which was about one mile from the campus. This group also conducted boys' clubs for the youth. St. Agnes Hospital and the kindergarten grew out of the community work as well.

COLLEGE PARK

ollege Park is bordered by Tarboro Street to the west, Oakwood Avenue to the north, Raleigh Boulevard to the east and New Bern Avenue to the west. The land that was originally subdivided for this area was the Fisher Farm, originally east of the Raleigh city limits, containing Lincoln Park to the south of New Bern Avenue and College Park to the north.

Kate Coke, widow of Colonel Octavius Coke, one-time secretary of state of North Carolina, owned the land after the death of her father. The land making up College Park was subdivided and purchased by D.J. Fort Jr. as early as 1912.

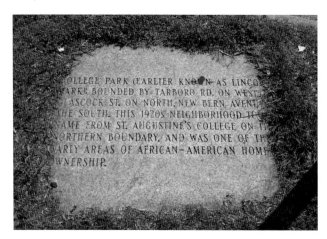

College Park stone marker, part of the city's Edenton New Bern History Walk, developed by North Central Community Advisory Council. *City of Raleigh.*

Many of the inhabitants, who were homeowners, worked at or had some connection to St. Augustine's College. Other occupations of the residents included janitors, butlers, porters, waiters, bricklayers and farmers.

Water and sewer lines were not provided for the residents of Lincoln Park or College Park, although residents of the area had been annexed and were assessed taxes for them. Attorney Fred J. Carnage, for whom a middle school in the city is named, took the petition that was drawn up and signed by the residents of the area and brought it before the General Assembly, forcing the city to approve the provision of water and sewer lines. This occurred in 1932.

SMOKY HOLLOW

S moky Hollow was a Black district to the north and west of the capital before the war. This area grew in the 1870s to 1880s. It was named Smoky Hollow because of the train smoke from the Raleigh and Gaston trains that would hang over the bottom land.

The neighborhood consisted of Tucker Street; Johnson Street; part of Harrington, West and Peace Streets; and Seaboard Station. Blacks lived in the 300 to 400 blocks of Tucker Street, and whites lived in the 500 to 600 blocks.

There was a hub of Black firemen and trained workers living in the area. According to an interview with Dr. Carl Devane for *Culture Town*, the folks who worked for the railroad lived well and had fine houses and big cars. They were able to purchase brand-new Hudson and Studebaker cars.

Mill and railroad workers also lived in the areas that were bordered by North Street, the railroad roundhouse, Johnson and Salisbury Streets, the Raleigh Cotton Mill and the Norfolk Southern Railway. This was considered the main part of the industrial district, including not only the railroad but also the railroad machine shops, two planing mills, a phosphate company and a foundry, so the area was an excellent source of good jobs for both Black and white people.

The firemen in the neighborhood were usually Black, but as the use of diesel engines increased, they were replaced by whites. Porters were normally Black. All conductors and engineers were white. The occupations for most of those working on the railroad included brick men, firemen, porters, railway mail clerks, cooks, waiters, clerks, orderlies, messengers and custodians. It

The weigh and transport site of the Raleigh and Gaston Railroad for the cotton yard of Raleigh Cotton Mill at the present site of the Legislative Building. *State Archives of North Carolina.*

was, however, rare for a Black man to be a railroad fireman. (This was not the same as a regular city fireman.) In Louis Dunbar's interview for *Culture Town*, he indicated that his father had this position.

Raleigh was the main thoroughfare for the Seaboard Airlines Railroad and the Raleigh Gaston Railroad. A good number of the employees came to Raleigh from other parts of the state because of the increase in pay due to the amount of travel with some of the jobs. Many of the men were able to purchase houses and other real estate.

There were some disputes between Blacks and whites. While the Black railroad men paid the same union dues as the whites, they were not allowed to participate in union activities such as fish fries and beer-drinking parties. Therefore, they had their own separate ones.

As diesel engines began to edge out the older coal engines, the unions would not allow Black men to work on those engines. If they were scheduled to work and the train coming in had a diesel engine, they were stalled until a white man came to the station to run it. They were allowed to shovel and throw coal into the fires to keep those engines running because the white employees could not handle the work, according to Jesse Dunbar's interview. He also said that it was important to have "pull" to get moved up the ladder or to have come from somewhere else. When he went to apply for a job, he was told to reference his father to get a better job.

Many of the Black railroad workers provided backing for the semipro baseball teams in the area. They bought balls and bats and provided uniforms for the players. These included Tom Scales, Jimmy Page and Connie Cagle. (More about these men and baseball in the section on recreation.)

RAILROAD WORKERS

Name	Railroad, if known	Notes	Job title, if known	Baseball team supporter
Adams, Porter				
Atkins, Jake				
Biscoe (East Martin Street)		1920 census, age 28; 1930 census, owned house worth $3,000; received pension in Montgomery County		
Brevard, Will				South Park
Burwell, L.S.	Southern RR			
Cagle, Connie (716 East Martin Street)	NS Railway	1910 census, age 18	Brakeman	East Raleigh
Carver, Coleman				
Dunbar (Louis's brother)				
Dunbar (Louis's father)	Seaboard RR Seaboard Coastline	62 years of service	Railway mail clerk; one of the first Black supervisors; carried a gun to work	
Dunbar, Louis		36.5 years of service	Laborer, wouldn't hire him as a fireman	

Name	Railroad, if known	Notes	Job title, if known	Baseball team supporter
Haywood, Lynn				
Haywood, Vernon				
Holmes				
McCullers, Charles				
Robinson				
Scales, Tom (212 Heck Street)		1942 city directory	Fireman	Idlewild
Wood, Joe				

The neighborhood was home to three predominantly black churches: First Baptist Church, which was on North Salisbury Street near the Raleigh and Gaston Railroad depot; St. Augustine's Episcopal Church, which shared land with the planing mill; and St. Paul AME Church, which was one block from the railroad. There were schools attached to the churches. The largest publicly funded school for Black children at the time was the Johnson School beside St. Paul AME Church.

The downtown area, where the Black population growth occurred, was an area desired by the white community. Black neighborhoods were often surrounded and choked out by the white community. In the 1880s, the white middle-class suburbs began to move into downtown from the west. Housing for millworkers, located adjacent to the mills, was only provided for white workers, not for Black ones.

Raleigh Cotton Mill was the first cotton mill built. It was next to the Raleigh and Gaston Railroad tracks. It started in 1890. African Americans were hired as custodians or warehousemen. It is now a condominium complex.

As part of the politics of the area, the Democrats accused Blacks of flooding the Fifth Ward in order to swing the election of 1875 in favor of the Republicans. The conservative media praised all of the white landlords and property owners who would not rent to Blacks, forcing them out of the area. This was the only ward not gerrymandered by the Democratic administration. In 1884, the final blow for saving the Black community was that the city school committee shut down the publicly funded Johnson School. The area was destroyed by urban renewal in the 1960s.

ST. PAUL AME CHURCH

In 1844, there was a split in the Methodist Episcopal Church denomination over the right of a Georgia bishop to own slaves. After the split, Edenton Street Church became part of the Methodist Episcopal Church, South. The enslaved membership of the church, which was growing rapidly, met in the basement of the building. After 1853, they relocated their worship services to the old Christ Episcopal Church building on the corner of New Bern Avenue and Wilmington Street.

Formally established in 1848, the congregation was named the African Church. In 1853, the white Methodists at Edenton Street purchased the building that had been used for the enslaved Black people's worship and put it in trust for them. In 1854, the slave membership physically moved the church building to the corner of Harrington and Edenton Streets, its present site, by rolling it down the street. From that time until 1865, the parent conference furnished white ministers and Sunday school teachers for the congregation. Reverend W.E. Pell (white) and Hardy Lockhart (Black) were the local preachers appointed by the Methodist Episcopal Conference for the group.

After Emancipation, in 1865, the members severed ties with Edenton Street and the Methodist Episcopal Conference. They joined the African Methodist Episcopal South Carolina Conference. They were known as the Loyal African Methodist Episcopal Church for twenty years and sometimes as the Lincoln Church because of a statue of the late president that was in the building. Their first Black pastor was Reverend George Broadie of Canada. In 1867, Edenton Street Methodist Church deeded the property on Harrington Street to the congregation. In 1884, the name of St. Paul African Methodist Episcopal Church was adopted. The church is considered the first independent Black congregation in Wake County and was the meeting site for the Freedmen's Conventions held during Reconstruction.

St. Paul AME Church was started in 1848 by slaves who were part of Edenton Street Methodist Church. It is at the corner of Edenton and Harrington Streets. *State Archives of North Carolina.*

ST. AMBROSE EPISCOPAL CHURCH

Reverend J. Brinton Smith, founder of St. Augustine's Normal School and Collegiate Institute (now St. Augustine's University), began conducting services in late December 1867 for what would later become St. Ambrose Episcopal Church. Ten people joined the church after separating from what was the likely integrated Christ Episcopal Church.

The church formally organized in February 1868, using the name St. Augustine's Protestant Episcopal Church, and met on the campus of the school. By act of the legislature in 1868, the church was granted use of a lot on the corner of Lane and Dawson Streets for ninety-nine years for a parochial school under the guidance of St. Ambrose, part of St. Augustine's Normal School. The church was renamed St. Ambrose so as not to be confused with the chapel that was on the campus. This was in the Smoky Hollow neighborhood.

St. Ambrose Episcopal Church, originally part of St. Augustine's College. It is presently located in historic Rochester Heights community. *State Archives of North Carolina.*

In 1868, education reformer Mary Phillips helped found the St. Ambrose School to help educate newly emancipated people. With an enrollment of 170 students, the church school had one of only four kindergarten programs in the state of North Carolina.

In the 1897 Session Laws of North Carolina, St. Ambrose's trustees were allowed to sell the land they had been granted to reinvest in other property for the same purposes. The land they acquired was on Wilmington and Cabarrus Streets, and the building on Dawson Street was physically moved to the new site. Renovation of the church included adding rooms in the basement (later used for social activities for youth) as well as a rectory (ministerial housing).

During the 1950s, the church became the first African American mission in the Episcopal Diocese of North Carolina to be a parish or self-supporting congregation. In 1965, the church relocated to its present site in the historic Rochester Heights neighborhood.

First Baptist Church

On March 7, 1812, First Baptist Church was organized by twenty-three people—fourteen enslaved and nine white. They were allowed to meet at the State House on the Capitol grounds, as were other churches in the immediate area. In 1816, they purchased their first building on Person Street between Hargett and Martin Streets. Six years later, they moved to a building on Moore Square, in an area that was then known as Baptist Grove. In 1844, the congregation moved to the corner of Wilmington and Morgan Streets on a lot purchased from Willie Jones.

The biracial congregation worshiped together for another twenty-two years until 1866. Separate Sunday afternoon services had been held since the mid-1850s, presumably to keep the races apart based on the law. After purchasing land from Jim Atkins, a Black member of the church, the group moved to the corner of Salisbury and Edenton Streets.

There was much dissatisfaction on the part of the Black members of the body because they had no say in the decision making of the church. In fact, they had to request an audience with the church board to speak. On June 5, 1868, Henry Jett asked for that permission and led two hundred Black members to request their own church and dismissal from the white body. This was granted. The minutes state:

As it was learned that a delegation from the colored church were at the door, on motion of Brother Pescud, they were received. Brother Henry Jett, one of those delegates, having expressed the thanks of the Church (colored) for some forms received from us and having made some remarks as to their condition and hopes state that the Colored Church wished our church to dismiss them in a body either by letter or by a singular vote. They having already organized in a separate body under the name of the colored led Baptist Church, on motion of Brother Mills, it was agreed that we recognize them as such. On motion of Brother Armstrong, Conference was adjourned by prayer.

They organized as First Colored Baptist Church. This group purchased a lot on North Salisbury Street between Johnson and North State Streets in the Smoky Hollow district. The first pastor was William Warrick of Pennsylvania. The new Black congregation worshiped at that site from 1868 until 1904. In 1896, they purchased back the former First Baptist Church property on the corner of Wilmington and Morgan Streets from the Roman Catholic Church of St. John the Baptist. First Baptist Church remains on that site today.

OLD FAIRGROUNDS

Old Fairgrounds was begun in 1873, when the North Carolina Agricultural Association moved the state fairgrounds to West Raleigh and sold the property. There were sixteen acres of property between Cotton Place and the Smith-Haywood neighborhood. Sixty-three small lots were created on the land that was there. That land was originally purchased by three men. John Gatling, who was an attorney, purchased nineteen lots. W.C. Stronach was a businessman, and M.A. Parker was an attorney.

All three men used the land for rental property. The remainder of the lots were purchased by white speculators. Real estate investors built cheap dwellings that they rented to the freedmen. All the lots were sold between 1873 and 1878. Twenty-one lots had been closed on in 1873. By 1880, fifty homes had been built across three streets.

MARTIN STREET BAPTIST CHURCH

Martin Street Baptist Church was formed in 1869 in the eastern part of Raleigh because the nearest church was one mile away. Members met in each other's homes until they were offered space to meet in the shoe shop of Mr. and Mrs. Virgil Anderson.

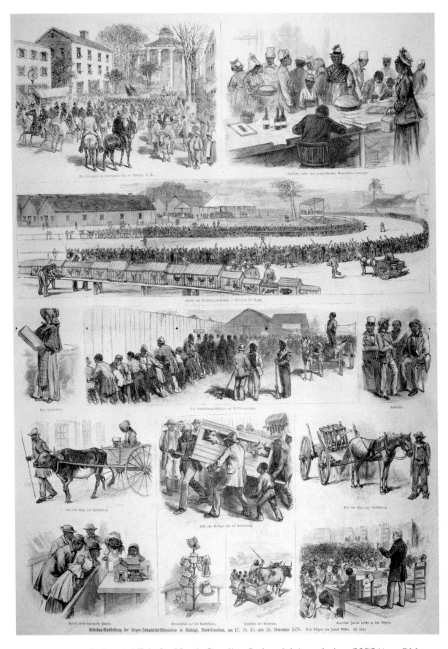

North Carolina Industrial Fair for North Carolina Industrial Association (NCIA) at Old Fairgrounds, 1879. This group was formed "to encourage and promote the development of the industrial and educational resources of the colored people of North Carolina." *State Archives of North Carolina.*

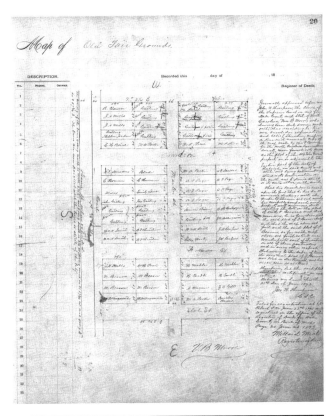

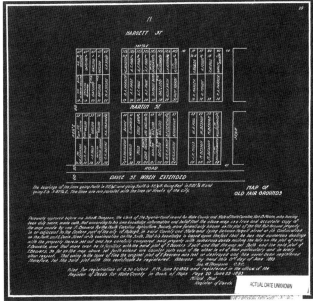

Top: A hand-drawn map of Old Fairgrounds with street crossings. The original map was lost, and an oath had to be sworn that these property boundaries were accurate. *Wake County Register of Deeds.*

Below: A county plotted map of Old Fairgrounds with street crossings. The original map was lost, and an oath had to be sworn that these property boundaries were accurate. *Wake County Register of Deeds.*

On a lot donated by Mrs. Anderson, the first church was built in the early 1870s on the south side of Martin Street between State Street and Tarboro Road. The first pastor was Reverend Thomas Edwards. Before this time, ministers from surrounding churches led the worship services.

Land was purchased for the new (and present) site in 1909, and the new building was begun in 1910. The congregation moved into the new building in 1919. Under the leadership of Reverend Elias Wimberley, a six-room parsonage was built on the site of the old church, across from the present site.

SMITH-HAYWOOD

The Smith-Haywood neighborhood was in East Raleigh around the Old Fairgrounds site. The boundaries were from Lenoir Street to East Street over to Davie Street, then to Tarboro Road over to Rock Quarry Road and back to Lenoir Street, just south of Cotton Place and east of St. Petersburg between Davie and Lenoir Streets.

In 1869, nine acres were purchased from the estate of James McKinnon by Reverend J. Brinton Smith, who was the white rector of St. Augustine's Episcopal Church and was also the headmaster of the Normal Institute at St. Augustine's. The other investor was Dr. Richard Haywood, a Raleigh physician. This acreage was subdivided into more than fifty small lots and sold primarily to freedmen. The area was located at the eastern end of Cabarrus Street. The streets were named for Smith and Haywood.

By 1872, eight houses had been built on Smith Street and sixteen houses on Haywood Street. There were twenty to thirty other houses in that vicinity. By 1881, twenty-six houses had been built on Smith Street and twenty houses on Haywood Street. In the early twentieth century, the area was called Lane's Bottom after Major George L. Lane.

Some of the Black residents included:
- Major George L. Lane, who owned a meat market and was a real estate developer
- Tony Burns, a restaurant owner
- Reuben Hodge, a farmer
- Robert Crossan, a police officer

507 South Bloodworth Street, built circa 1850. *Author photo.*

316 East Cabarrus Street, built circa 1909. *Author photo.*

501 East Cabarrus Street, built circa 1925. *Author photo.*

- Allen Lane and Henry Marshall, both stonecutters
- Steven and Winnie Worth, freed slaves of former governor Jonathan Worth

Some of the white residents were:

- S.N. Whelson, a merchant
- Eliza Reeves, a widow
- W.N. Harris, a grocer

Haywood Street, the Smith-Haywood area, St. Petersburg and Cotton Place represented a mix of social groups and races. The white residents also included merchants and skilled craftsmen. They built homes along Martin, Haywood, Swain and Hargett Streets.

MAJOR GEORGE L. LANE

Major George L. Lane was born a slave in 1840. He was of mixed blood. His wife, Adeline Virginia Dunn, was born in 1843. They married after the Civil War. He was twenty-five and she was twenty-two. They had ten children.

Major Lane was an entrepreneur. He made furniture, built coffins and was the first Black undertaker in Raleigh. His mortuary was on Salisbury Street. People were not embalmed very often at that time. He was also a stonecutter. He was known as one of the quarry freedmen, along with Tom Williams. They helped to build the Capitol on Union Square.

Major Lane was one of the most prominent landlords and developers in the area. He built lots of small houses and rented them out. (The area the houses were in was off Davie Street and Alston Avenue. It was named Smith Street at the time and known as Lane's Bottom.)

Major Lane built his home at 728 East Davie Street; it is no longer standing. The stairwells were made by hand and turned. They were made of mahogany wood. The house was white with big pillars in front. There was a fireplace in each room. The house was of frame construction with six rooms downstairs, a bath and two rooms upstairs. He owned a general store that was attached to the house.

Major Lane was very much an education advocate. This is what drove him to help to find land for Davie Street Parochial School, later Davie Street Presbyterian Church, where he was a member. All of his children were educated and completed college. Most of them had professional degrees. His family has a long history in the city of Raleigh.

His son Charles graduated from Shaw University and attended Lincoln University, where he became a doctor. He settled in St. Louis. However, during the race riots in St. Louis, many Black professionals were killed, and he was never heard from after the riots. Son George graduated from Shaw University and also attended Lincoln. He received his law degree and returned to Raleigh. He was the first Black person to pass the state bar exam, in 1905. He had an office on Martin Street.

WATSON'S ADDITION

I n 1891, John W.B. Watson died. Between 1895 and 1897, the heirs of the John W.B. Watson farm divided his land into hundreds of narrow lots for rental housing in southeast Raleigh. There were eight separate parcels of land divided. They were:

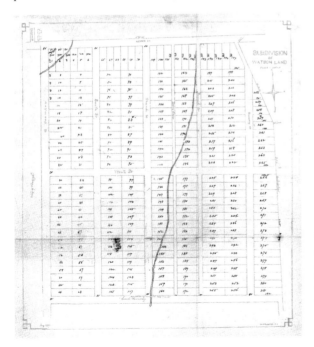

Watson's Land Addition #1 of 1896 created a new city southern boundary. The land from Lenoir to Worth Streets includes Haywood, Smith, Church, Branch and Quarry. *Wake County Register of Deeds.*

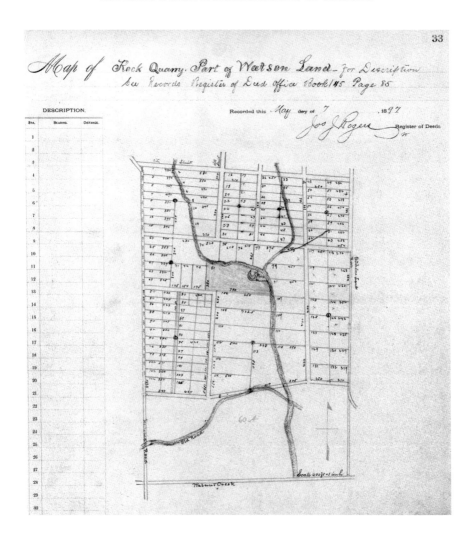

Above: Rock Quarry Watson Addition of 1897 extended the city southward. The rock quarry at the back of Lucille Hunter School provided stone for the state capitol. *Wake County Register of Deeds.*

Opposite: Watson's Land Addition of 1898. This map shows the topography of land, including Haywood, Smithfield, Matthews and McMakin Streets. *Wake County Register of Deeds.*

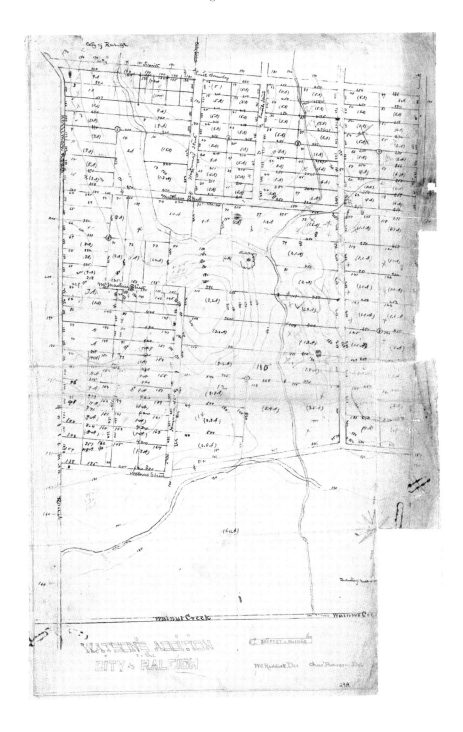

WATSON LANDS

Date Recorded in Register of Deeds Office	Property Description	Boundaries
July 23, 1895	Jno W.B. Watson Property in City of Raleigh	Bordered by East Davie Street on north; South Swain Street on east; East Cabarrus Street on south; and including Watson and Green Streets
	Total of 38 lots platted with structures on 7	
	Platted and surveyed by A.W. Shaffer, May 1895	
July 23, 1895	Watson's Addition to the City of Raleigh	Bordered by East Lenoir Street on north; East Boundary Street on east; South Boundary and Smithfield Streets on south; includes East South, East Worth and South Bloodworth Streets
	Total of 61 lots platted and surveyed by A.W. Shaffer in May 1895	
	Site of Deaf, Dumb and Blind Asylum for Colored shown in upper left of map	

Date Recorded in Register of Deeds Office	Property Description	Boundaries
	Mineral Springs Branch and Watson Spring Branch included on map	
August 1896	Subdivision of Watson Land	Bordered by Lenoir Street to north; South Boundary Street to south and an extension of the southern city limit; Haywood Street to the west; includes Smith, Church, Branch, Worth and Quarry Streets and Davy Lane
	265 lots platted by W.C. Riddick, civil engineer, on first page; 281 lots platted on second page	
	two unnamed tributaries cross the land	
December 14, 1896	Topographical map showing southern boundary extension for City of Raleigh surveyed and platted by W.C. Riddick for estate of J.W.B. Watson; 153 lots platted.	Land shown bordered by southern boundary of Raleigh city limits to the north and Holleman Road to the west. Walnut Creek to the south, with two unnamed tributaries running in a forked shape through the property. Streets included are Haywood, Smithfield, McMakin, Walnut and Mathews.

Date Recorded in Register of Deeds Office	Property Description	Boundaries
May 7, 1897	Rock quarry part of Watson Land	Bordered by southern city limits to north, Batchelor's land to east, Walnut Creek to south and Holleman Road to west.
	Same map as December 14, 1896, without topographical outlines	
	Clearly shows rock quarry at fork between two tributaries	
April 21, 1909	Maynard D. Watson Property, deeded to Raleigh Real Estate & Trust Co.	Bordered by Lenoir Street to north, graded school to east, Chavis Way to west with South and Wynne Street inside borders crossed by Worth's Fish Pond Branch.
December 28, 1909	Map of Quarry Hill	Bordered by Rock Quarry Road, Quarry Street, southern city limits and railroad right of way.
	Map showing lots platted between Quarry, Coleman, Vardaman and Page Streets over to Rock Quarry Road. Also shown is site of quarry between Lenoir, Quarry and Coleman Streets and Rock Quarry Road.	

Date Recorded in Register of Deeds Office	Property Description	Boundaries
	Brill Branch and eastern city limits shown as well.	
No date given	Watson property inside city limits	Bordered by Lenoir and Haywood Streets.
	Shows Crosby school property and position of land where Chavis Memorial Park sits. Also shows Boundary Branch.	

Much of the property went for rental and tract housing, otherwise known as shotgun houses. They were listed as tenements on the fire and insurance maps. The properties were spread over a four-block area in southeast Raleigh. These were long and narrow gable-ended forms, one room wide and three rooms deep. They were generally fifteen feet by thirty feet with a wide front porch.

One of the major developers and landlords in this area was E.A. Johnson, a Black attorney and the principal at Washington Graded School. He was also an author and the first dean of Shaw University's Law School. He owned one hundred rental units, including fourteen shotgun homes on a one-block span of South Bloodworth Street. The other major developer was Milford Gurley, who was a white realtor. Many of the homes in Fourth Ward that he owned were double shotguns, serving two families.

In 1897, the Crosby Colored Graded School was established in the former Watson mansion on Lenoir Street. The area surrounding the school became one of the city's largest Black neighborhoods. Most of the land in the eastern half of South Raleigh was owned by the Watsons. The land that wasn't part of the first group of subdivisions to be sold and built was kept intact until the mid-1880s.

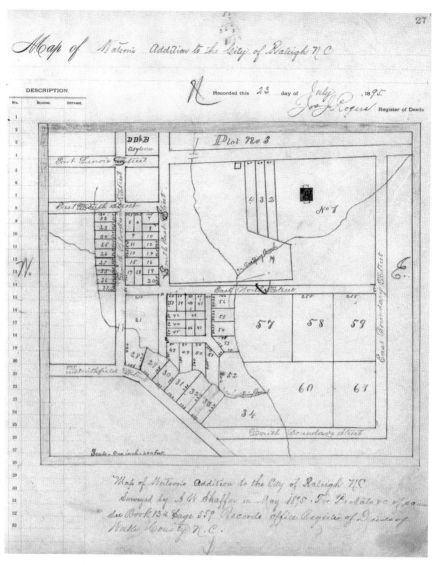

Above: Watson's Land Addition of 1895 shows the site of the Deaf, Dumb and Blind Asylum, as well as several creek branches. *Wake County Register of Deeds.*

Opposite: Watson's Land inside city boundaries. The top middle box is Crosby Garfield School. The large plot at the bottom of the map would eventually become Chavis Memorial Park. *Wake County Register of Deeds.*

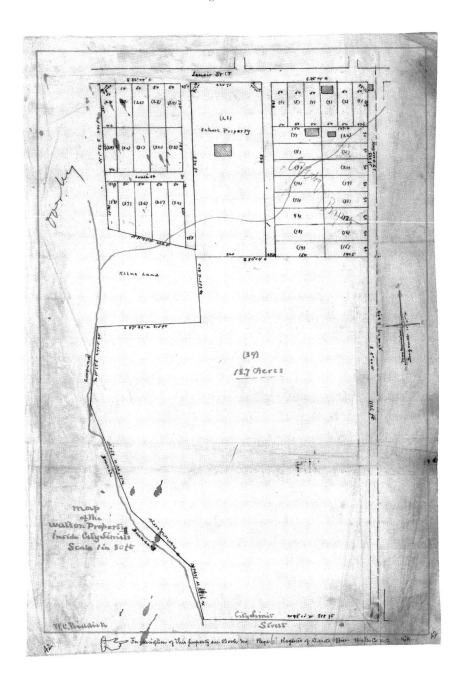

SOUTH PARK/EAST RALEIGH

T he South Park/East Raleigh neighborhood includes Battery Heights, Chavis Heights, Cotton Place, St. Petersburg and Third Ward. It is also made up of portions of the historic neighborhoods of Smith-Haywood that developed after the Civil War. The main street borders are East Hargett Street to the north; Bragg, Branch and East Lenoir Street to the south; Camden, South Swain and South East Streets to the east; and South Blount and South Wilmington Streets to the west.

The National Historic Register document dated October 11, 1990, that designates the South Park/East Raleigh area of significant interest states:

> It is on all four parts of forty-eight blocks east and southeast of the central business district of Raleigh. It's considered one of the largest and most historically relatively intact urban Black residential and cultural concentrations in North Carolina. The significant periods of time for this neighborhood were 1850 to 1855 and 1865 to 1941. However, few of the buildings are designated as local historic buildings and so many were not saved from destruction. During the application for the historic designation seventy-five percent of the structures or five hundred thirty-two of seven hundred are for rent or identified as contributing structures, but many of these have been torn down.

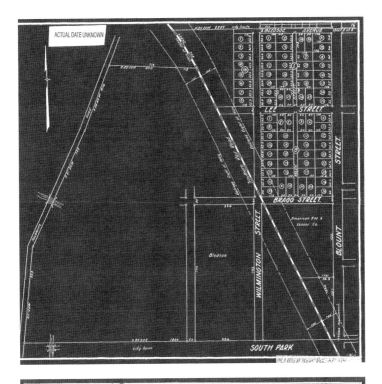

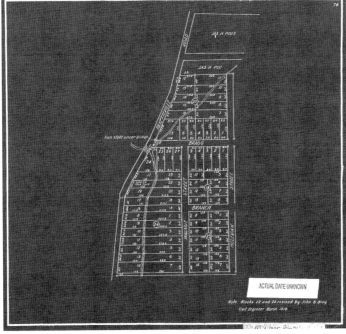

Top: South Park plat map #2 from Wilmington Street through Blount Street. *Wake County Register of Deeds.*

Bottom: South Park plat map #3 from Fayetteville Street to Holleman Street showing the area of future Walnut Terrace. *Wake County Register of Deeds.*

SOUTH PARK

South Park was home to the professional class of Blacks who owned businesses, pastored churches, worked in government or industry or served as educational or civic leaders in the community. The area is grouped based on relationships to educational, governmental and commercial environments in downtown Raleigh.

South Park began to develop in the early 1900s, but the most intense growth came after 1930. The area is bounded by Bledsoe, Hoke, East and Wilmington Streets. In 1907, ads placed by the Raleigh Real Estate and Trust Company asked people to buy lots in South Park. In a fifteen-block subdivision, 122 house lots were sold. In 1910, several streets were lined with owner-occupied shotgun homes, cottages and two-room dwellings. Many were built for workers at the nearby American Veneer and Box Company.

The neighborhood was developed by the white-owned Raleigh Real Estate Company, which had purchased the Moses Bledsoe property to develop as Black suburbs. The area was south of the original city limits. The development was encouraged by attorney and Shaw Law School dean Edward A. Johnson. The land was located south of Shaw University, and people were able to get no-interest mortgages. There was also streetcar

Historic South Park sign at the corner of South East Street and Martin Luther King Boulevard. *Author photo.*

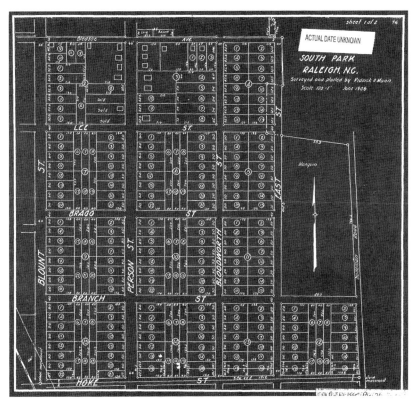

South Park plat map #1 that shows the boundaries of Blount Street, Bledsoe Avenue, East Street and Hoke Street with Lee, Person, Bloodworth, Bragg and Branch Streets. *Wake County Register of Deeds.*

GRAND OPPORTUNITY.

To speculate in a small way. Don't buy a vacant lot or house and lot until you see what we have to offer. We have some bargains. Money invested in "South Park" lots will be sure to double in a short while. We can sell you a lot by paying $10.00 down and $5.00 a month until paid for. No interest charged.

FOR RENT.

6 room house, modern conveniences, Harp Street.
9 room house, modern conveniences, East Jones Street.
12 room house, modern conveniences, Boylan Avenue.

RALEIGH REAL ESTATE AND TRUST COMPANY
130 Fayetteville Street.

A South Park rental/investment ad for property to purchase or rent. *From the* Raleigh Times, *October 31, 1907.*

The state constitution (1868) provided for a "colored Department" of the state school for the blind and deaf (1873) housed on Bloodworth and Lenoir Streets. It became the YMCA and was then acquired by Shaw University. *The Albert Barden Collection, State Archives of North Carolina.*

service provided. Much of the development of the area came from those at Second Baptist Church (which became Tupper Memorial), Shaw Collegiate Institute (which became Shaw University) and the School for the Colored Deaf, Dumb and Blind.

EAST RALEIGH

East Raleigh was the area of Raleigh beyond East Street that went past today's Richard B. Harrison Library on New Bern Avenue. It was a fashionable white area before the Civil War and became the focus for Black settlements after the war ended. By the end of the war, freedmen were already settling around the Old Fairgrounds area.

RUSH METROPOLITAN CHURCH

Rush Metropolitan Church remains on its original site as established in 1882. The building was reconstructed in 1938 on the same site. It is believed that the builder was a Black man from Franklinton named Mr. Blackwell. The church was named after Bishop Christopher Rush, who was born into slavery in Craven County, a seaport community 115 miles southeast of Raleigh.

CALVIN A. LIGHTNER

Calvin A. Lightner, originally from South Carolina, came to Raleigh to attend Shaw University. He was on the first football team at Shaw and eventually became a coach.

He began a construction business in 1908. He married in 1909, and his wife, who had attended Fayetteville State and Hampton Institute, taught home economics in the Raleigh public school system. He attempted to start his business earlier but had problems getting a charter and had to fight the issue in court. In 1911, he received the official charter and began a funeral home business. Prior to starting the funeral home, he had been a builder in the area. His family were farmers in South Carolina, as well as builders and contractors. He built most of the Colonial homes that were in the Black community in Raleigh. He was not an architect but could draw and create blueprints.

He built Davie Street Presbyterian Church and the original Mechanics and Farmers building. He built an office at 110 East Hargett Street. Calvin Lightner built the Lightner Building in 1915. The ground floor of the building had a cleaner and pressing shop, as well as a barbershop. On the second level were professional offices for doctors and dentists, as well as beauty parlors. There were apartments on the top floor.

In 1921, he built the Lightner Arcade at 120 East Hargett Street. The ground floor had a barbershop, drugstore and restaurant. Large buildings at that time didn't have steel in them but used bead wood and trusses. The building stood until the 1940s, when it was torn down. The arcade was a place where noted Blacks could stay in between Washington, D.C., and Florida, which was hard to come by during that time. Some famous people who stayed in the hotel included Cab Calloway, Duke Ellington and Count Basie. Many other bands stayed there as well.

There were also boardinghouses over in Smoky Hollow near the Pine State Dairy, the Harris boardinghouse in the 400 block of Blount Street, the Lewis Hotel on Cabarrus Street, the Starksvilla Guest House on Bragg Street and a couple of other smaller boardinghouses in the area.

It was not necessarily Calvin Lightner's intention to become a mortician or own a funeral home. In an interview, his son Clarence Lightner told this story. Calvin was building a house on Fayetteville Crossing behind River Street Baptist Church. Brown Funeral Home was burying Blacks at the time because there was no Black funeral home. Mr. Brown asked if someone could help unload six people and take them into the church.

Lightner Arcade (1921), built by Calvin Lightner at 122 East Hargett Street. It was the main location of social activity for Blacks and included a ballroom, meeting space and hotel rooms. *State Archives of North Carolina.*

Lightner noticed that he had a one-horse wagon and chairs for people to ride in; there were no cars at the time.

The next time Lightner saw Brown was at a white funeral. The white people had coaches and four black horses provided for them. Lightner did not like the difference in treatment between Blacks and whites, so he decided to start a funeral business.

The business started in a wooden frame house on Hargett Street. He gave up the construction business for the funeral business. Calvin Lightner took a six-week course and exam in order to become a mortician from what is now Brown-Wynne Funeral Home. Eventually, the business moved to the location on Smithfield Street (purchased from Dr. Lovelace Capehart), which is now Martin Luther King Boulevard.

Lightner ran for city commissioner in the 1920s. He was one of the first Blacks in the city to run for office. He ran on the same ticket with Dr. Manassa Pope and Bob Seneca, who was a newspaper editor. White people tried to put them all out of business for running for office. However, Lightner made his own embalming fluid, and his business was able to survive. This was an issue because the white merchants would not sell any of these men items needed for their business.

Calvin Lightner also owned a farm on Garner Road past Walnut Creek near Hillcrest Cemetery (which was part of the funeral home). He had about two hundred acres of land. Eventually, the land was sold from his estate, first for the Rochester Heights development and then for Biltmore Hills. Three of the Lightner families lived on the farm. There was a dairy on the property, as well as a pig farm. The families also raised corn, cotton and tobacco.

During the Depression, Lightner lost a great deal of property. He was able to keep his home at 419 South East Street, the farm and a couple of other places. His wife did hair during the Depression to help with family expenses as well as send their children to college. She also worked in the cafeteria at Lucille Hunter School and taught music. They had four living children; two died at birth. The other children were Lawrence, Nicholas Calvin III, Margaret and Clarence, who would go on to become Raleigh's first Black mayor.

WILMINGTON-BLOUNT

I n the Wilmington-Blount corridor, around the east side of Shaw University, one- and two-story frame houses were occupied by both Black and white families. By 1890, the area was called Faculty Row.

ERNESTINE PEGUES HAMLIN

Ernestine Pegues Hamlin was born in 1890 across the street from Shaw University on the corner of Wilmington and Worth Streets. She was born at home because there was no hospital at the time. This information is from her interview for *Culture Town*.

Her father, Albert Witherspoon Pegues, was from South Carolina. He left home at the age of twelve to go to public school. He completed school and left to go to Virginia, where he attended Virginia Union, and then he came to Shaw University. He taught religion at Shaw and also taught at the Colored School for the Deaf, Dumb and Blind.

When Mrs. Hamlin was growing up, the family doctor was Dr. Manassa Pope. She isn't sure if he delivered her or not. She was friends with his daughters. She remembers that there was a white public school where Memorial Auditorium sits today (Centennial School). There was also a missionary training school run by white people. They taught and lived in a house on Wilmington Street.

Hamlin recalled Shaw University students playing football and baseball in front of her house on Wilmington Street. She states that when they first moved to the house on South Street, the street was a mud hole. Her father had the street fixed.

There was often entertainment at Shaw University. Sometimes the students would perform, and sometimes children in the community would perform. The entertainment could be operas or musical entertainment. There was natural seating on the lawn in front of Estey Hall. As a child growing up, she played in Estey Hall. There were no neighbors close by.

Students were not allowed to smoke on the campus. She recalls the medical students throwing their cigarette butts down in the street just before entering the gates of the school.

She attended the Chavis School and only remembers that it was "way out." She walked to school. After she left Chavis, she attended Washington School. Hamlin finished high school at Shaw University. Cooking was taught on the top floor of Estey Hall and sewing taught on the second floor.

During the time that she was growing up, people were killed at the prison by hanging as opposed to electrocution. If they didn't have family, their bodies were brought to Leonard Medical School for use as cadavers. Hamlin would go upstairs to her room, which was on the back side of the house, and watch as the students practiced operating, performing autopsies and surgery.

Dr. Pegues bought the house that the family lived in when he became dean of the Shaw School of Religion from the Josephus Daniels family. Josephus Daniels, editor of the *News and Observer* at the time, described Shaw University as "commanding the heart of the Negro District." This house, on South Street, across from the front gates of Shaw University, is known as the Bagley-Daniels-Pegues-Hamlin House. Dr. Pegues left the house to Mrs. Hamlin. He also had property in New York City.

She said that she was the first colored girl to drive a car in Raleigh. Her daddy paid somebody to teach her how to drive. The car she owned was a Paige, made by a company in Detroit. Paiges were luxury cars sold between 1908 and 1927. Her car could seat seven or nine passengers. She said that three people could sit in the front, three in the back and you could pull two seats down from the front in order to get more in the car. She would drive her friends all over Raleigh. On Sunday afternoons, she and her mother would drive to Franklinton to pick her father up from the church that he pastored. Dr. Pope bought a Paige car after they did.

Her friends included Willie Otey, Mildred Taylor, Lizzie Constance, Martha Wheeler and Chloe Laws. Both Willie Otey and Mildred Taylor

Bagley-Daniels-Pegues-Hamlin House, home of Josephus Daniels and Ernestine Hamlin. Her father was dean of Shaw's School of Theology, and her husband was the pharmacist-owner of Community Drug Store. It is across from Shaw University. *Author photo.*

sewed (as did Lizzie Constance). Martha Wheeler taught at Shaw University and was the registrar at one point.

After attending Shaw for two years, Hamlin left and went to Cheyney, Pennsylvania, where she studied home economics. Upon her return to Raleigh, she taught at the Deaf and Blind School. She worked with the deaf and dumb children and preferred not to work with the blind children. She taught the children to spell by using their hands on their vocal cords to sound out the letters. Later, she taught the deaf girls how to cook.

Her husband, Dr. Tom Hamlin, started the pharmacy program at Leonard School of Pharmacy at Shaw University. However, the school closed before he finished. He graduated from Howard University Pharmacy School. After Tom served in the U.S. Navy, the Hamlins moved to West Virginia. Dr. Hamlin had a drugstore in West Virginia called Community Drug Store. After a couple of years, they returned to Raleigh.

They opened Community Drug Store on Hargett Street and both worked in the store. At that time, there were two drugstores on Hargett Street: Hamlin on one side and Community Drug on the other. Mrs. Hamlin felt that they were wasting money paying rent on Hargett Street when they owned property on Blount Street. After convincing her husband of that fact, they tore down the horse stable that was on the Blount Street property and built there. (The author's father purchased that drugstore from the Hamlins and ran it for forty-three years.)

Hamlin also reminisced about working in various offices at Shaw University, including the offices of the president, registrar and the Alumni Department. She and her husband had two children.

SOUTH PARK/WATSON'S ADDITION SELECTED HOMEOWNERS

Street Address	Owner's Name	Occupation	Notes
114 East Lenoir Street	Arthur L. Gorham	postal carrier	house moved to 420 South Bloodworth Street, now boutique hotel called Guest House
223 East Lenoir Street	Dr. Peter H. Williams	physician	graduated Leonard Medical School
573 East Lenoir Street	Dr. John W. Ligon	educator, preacher, community activist	
312 Smithfield Street	Dr. Lovelace B. Capehart/ Lightner Funeral Home	Dr. Capehart was physician and educator	Calvin Lightner purchased the Capehart home for Lightner Funeral Home; Smithfield Street is now Martin Luther King Boulevard
213 East Cabarrus Street	Jones-Williams		constructed by Lucius Wilcox, Black builder
312 East Cabarrus Street	Leonidas Frazier		
542 East Cabarrus Street	William Jones/ Adolphus Barrett		

Street Address	Owner's Name	Occupation	Notes
571 East Cabarrus Street	John W. Ligon	Ligon Store	
573 East Cabarrus			
575 East Cabarrus Street	Bilyeu-Ligon		
604/604½ East Cabarrus Street			house and attached store
121 East South Street	Charles Frazier	cashier for Mechanic & Farmers Bank; secretary-treasurer for Capital Building and Loan Association	
125 East South Street	Reverend Albert Pegues/Dr. Tom and Ernestine P. Hamlin	Pegues: dean, Shaw School of Religion; president, Union Publishing; vice president, Capital Building Loan Association; pharmacist and owner, Community Drug Store	
316 East South Street	Reverend Cicero Pope	Shaw University teacher	

Street Address	Owner's Name	Occupation	Notes
318 East South Street	Gaston A. Edwards/ Reverend W. Watkins	architect, taught at State School for Deaf, Dumb and Blind (colored), taught at Shaw University, designed Tyler Hall (1910) at Shaw University, Supervisor of Men's Industrial Department at Shaw/taught at Shaw University (1925)	
406 East South Street	Thomas and Stella Burgess		
511 South Wilmington Street	Dr. Manassas Pope	physician	graduated Leonard Medical School
316 South Haywood Street	Charles G. Williams	attorney	
425 South Haywood Street	A.J. Rogers	cashier for North Carolina Mutual Life Insurance Company	
419 South East Street	Calvin Lightner	contractor and funeral home director	graduated Shaw University
723 South East Street	Frank Killebrew		

Street Address	Owner's Name	Occupation	Notes
720 South East Street	Charles A. "Doll" Haywood	filling station manager; Raleigh Funeral Home director; owner, Haywood Funeral Home	
724 South East Street	W.J. Latham/ Mabel and Louise Latham	janitor at Wiley School; educators and community activist	Louise Latham began the Raleigh Chapter of Women in Action for the Prevention of Violence and Its Causes in 1971 with its corresponding telephone referral service (A Call to Action) to direct citizens to proper sources for help with consumer and other problems
802 South East Street	George W. Greene/ Top Greene/ Lonnette Williams	George Greene: cleaner and dyer at Raleigh French Cleaning and Drying Company; Top Greene: Tuskegee airman, Haywood Funeral Home, community activist; Lonnette Williams: educator, community activist	

Street Address	Owner's Name	Occupation	Notes
812 South East Street	Dr. Lovelace B. Capehart	physician and educator	graduated Leonard Medical School
905 South East Street	Joseph G. Mordecai	drayman	
408 South Bloodworth Street	Dr. and Mrs. Richard E. Wimberley	pharmacist	graduate of Bricks School, Enfield; attended Leonard Medical School, graduated from Meharry College
518 South Bloodworth Street	Frank W. Cumbo	barber	Cumbo Barber Shop
800 South Bloodworth Street	Seth and Mary Barber	home and grocery store attached	
909 South Bloodworth Street	Thomas and Nannie Clark	cook	
915 South Bloodworth Street	Royal E. Dunston	plasterer	
916 South Bloodworth Street	Samuel and Odessa Roberts	bricklayer	
1006 South Person Street	Reverend Henry C. Nunn	pastor	
1013 South Person Street	Ferry Noble/ William Allen/ Louis H. Roberts/Samuel C. Harris	Noble (barber); Roberts (dept. mgr.); Harris (barber, founder of Harris Barber College); parsonage for Fayetteville Street Baptist Church	

Street Address	Owner's Name	Occupation	Notes
1014 South Person Street	Samuel C. Harris	barber, founder of Harris Barber College	
1103 South Person Street	Samuel B. Haywood	student	
600 South Blount Street	Hamlin/ Wimberley	Community Drug Store	originally on Hargett Street
803 South Blount Street	Samuel C. Harris		Harris Barber College
902 South Blount Street	Eugene Logan	secretary of Progressive Real Estate	
1106 South Blount Street	Henry and John Evans	carpenters	
601/603 East Martin Street		home and grocery store attached	
317 Worth Street		home and grocery store attached	
510 Worth Street	William and Alvise DeVane	William (patrolman); Alvise (teacher)	Dr. Carl Devane, political science professor at Shaw University, Howard University, Washington, D.C.
404 Bledsoe Avenue	Thomas C. Hayes	plasterer	
406 Bledsoe Avenue	Pace House		family lived there for over seventy years
210 East Lee Street	Hurley A. Jones	bricklayer	

Shaw University

The history of Shaw University is irrevocably intertwined with the story of Dr. Henry M. Tupper. Dr. Tupper was a Union army soldier and Yankee Baptist minister. He was consistently engaged in Christian work by holding meetings with the soldiers and performing the duties of a chaplain. During his time in the war, he became well acquainted with the colored people who came to camp, and he studied their needs and conditions. He was discharged from the army on July 14, 1865. Prior to his discharge, he went before the officers of the American Baptist Home Mission Society in New York and requested to be sent as a missionary to the freedmen of the South. Originally, he had wanted to go to Africa, but after hosting a large Sunday school class of colored youth, the South was his second choice. He was allowed to be a missionary to formerly enslaved people, but he had to choose his own field.

He and his new bride traveled on their honeymoon to Raleigh, North Carolina, and determined that this was where their mission field would be. After introducing himself to the Baptist preacher, Tupper asked permission to teach the formerly enslaved people who met in the church basement and was denied. There was generally no place to gather people for religious instruction except for under a tree or in the dark cabins where people lived. He began a class for adult ministers in the Guion Hotel. His wife held a class for women in a private home. Eventually, he started teaching in a cabin on the outskirts of the city. He and his helpers went into the woods to cut down trees and hew logs to build the first building.

The need for assistance for the people was great. Most of them were poor and destitute. Many of them were refugees who had followed the army after the war ended and were now "houseless and homeless." Dr. Tupper was able to aid people in getting food and clothing from the Freedmen's Bureau. At one point, he had a list of 175 people who were over the age of seventy-five whom he was able to assist in getting provisions.

After a short time, he requested permission from the society to purchase a site for building. The building would be two stories, one for the church and the other for the school. On February 17, 1866, he organized a church and paid $500 that he had saved, while he was a soldier, for a piece of land at the corner of Blount and Cabarrus Streets. The land was purchased on February 23.

It cost $1,300 to construct the first story of the building. In October 1866, the school was opened with three teachers who were from the New England Freedmen's Aid Society. The school had 250 day students and 109 night students, with funding also coming partially from the Freedmen's Bureau. Over the first four years the school was in session, more than 1,000 men, women and children attended.

In the spring of 1867, the second story was added to the building. The cost of purchasing the lot and building the facility was $6,500; $3,800 was raised in the North, $2,400 was given by the Freedmen's Bureau and $300 was contributed by the "colored people."

The name of the school was the Raleigh Theological Institute. There was a three-month school session. The first session, there were fifteen pupils who boarded at a cost of $129.52. The Freedmen's Bureau gave $0.25 a month per pupil toward the cost of the teachers. The Peabody Fund gave the same amount.

Dr. Henry M Tupper, a Union army soldier, started Second Baptist Church (Tupper Memorial Baptist Church) and Raleigh Institute (Shaw University). *From* A Narrative of Twenty-Five Years' Work in the South *by Henry Lyman Morehouse.*

By 1870, the school had outgrown the building. Dr. Tupper tried to purchase Peace Institute, but the sale was called off when it was found that it would be used for a colored school. In 1870, Dr. Tupper was able to purchase the Daniel Barringer estate at a cost of $1,300. This property is located on South Street between Wilmington and Blount Streets. The neighborhood was south of the old Governor's Mansion, which became Centennial School and eventually Memorial Auditorium. It was east of the North Carolina Railroad and abutted the southern city limits at the Bledsoe property.

Elijah Shaw, a wool manufacturer in Wales, Massachusetts, donated $5,000 to the cause. The Freedmen's Bureau gave $4,000. The remaining amount was raised from Tupper solicitations. Elijah Shaw loaned the school $3,000 in order to make the bricks to build the school buildings. Eventually, that loan became a donation. The students made one million bricks from the clay on the campus. The bricks that were not used in the school's building were sold at a profit of $3,475.74.

Shaw Hall was built near the spot where Grant conferred with Sherman on the terms of surrender of the Confederate troops. Ironically, this was

FOUNDED 1865   INCORPORATED 1870

Forty-fourth Annual Catalogue of
the Officers and Students

OF

SHAW UNIVERSITY

RALEIGH, N. C.

For the Academic Year Ending May Thirty-first
Nineteen Hundred and Eighteen

RALEIGH, N. C.
EDWARDS & BROUGHTON PRINTING CO.
1918

Above: Shaw Hall, named for Elijah Shaw, the Massachusetts donor whose funds enabled Dr. Tupper to purchase the Daniel Barringer estate on which Shaw University sits today. *State Archives of North Carolina.*

Left: The cover of the 1918 Shaw University catalogue printed by Edwards & Broughton Printing Company. *DigitalNC, State Library of North Carolina.*

Commencement of the Leonard School of Medicine and Pharmacy and Law Department at Shaw, Friday Evening April 2.

The beautiful college chapel by 8:30 o'clock was filled with one of the most intelligent looking audiences we have seen, to witness the exercises of the evening. Rev. H. L. Wayland, D. D., of Philadelphia, was introduced by President Meserve, to deliver the address to the graduating class. The address was in every particular practical and eloquent.

Hon. Walter Clark, Associate Justice of the Supreme Court, awarded the diplomas. He, in a short speech, congratulated the colored people upon the rapid strides they have made since their emancipation in education. President Meserve delivered the parting address to the graduates and presented the prizes. Haywood's Orchestra furnished some excellent music.

Graduates in Medicine—David Newton Emanuel Campbell, Jamaica, West Indies; Garland Alphonso Gerran, North Carolina; Joseph Clinton Hood, Ph. B., North Carolina; William Henry Hughes, Jr., A. B., Virginia; John Quincy McDougald, North Carolina; Nelson Frederck McNorton, Virginia; Allen Atkins Wyche, North Carolina.

Graduates in Pharmacy — Edward Thomas Hasty, North Carolina; John Henry Harris, North Carolina; Walter Louis McNair, North Carolina; Earnest Clopton Merchant, Virginia; Charles Wesley Morris, Virginia; John Willis Satterwhite, South Carolina; William Henry Vick, A. B., North Carolina; Miss Pearle Rudolph Wassom, B. S., Tennessee.

Graduates in Law.—John Alfred Gaillard, South Carolina; Frank Marion Kennedy, Tennessee; Mark Anderson Williams, North Carolina.

One of the distinguished features of the commencement exercises was that no speeches were made by the graduates, and all the members of the graduating class wore caps and gowns.

Among the distinguished visitors attending the commencement, we noticed Hon. E. E. Smith, Principal of the State Normal School, Fayetteville; Prof. S. H. Vick, of Wilson; Dr. M T. Pope, of Charlotte; Dr. George Williams, of Wilson; Rev. P. F. Maloy, of Greensboro.

An article with the details of graduates from Shaw University and its professional schools in 1897. *From the* Gazette, *April 1897.*

the site of the cotton fields where Dr. Tupper and his wife hid from lynch mobs after it was found that he was teaching formerly enslaved people.

Shaw University was considered the center of learning for future ministers, teachers, nurses, pharmacists, lawyers and medical doctors. The university atmosphere also provided academic, cultural and recreational opportunities for members of the community.

According to Dr. Wilmoth Carter in her book *Shaw's Universe*, it was not incidental that Reconstruction started in the schoolhouse rather than the state house.

Families began to come to the neighborhood where the school was located. Across the street to the east, one- and two-story frame houses were occupied by both Black and white families. In the 1890s, the area was known as Faculty Row for Shaw employees.

Shaw built a ballpark that the public also used as a field to play ball. They had football and baseball teams. According to Mrs. Ernestine P. Hamlin, plays and productions that were opened to the public were given on the front lawn of the school. By the 1890s, the campus was ten acres in size and had six buildings. One of those buildings was Estey Hall. It was the seminary and dormitory for women, as well as a classroom building. It also held the Baptist chapel. Estey Hall was named for Colonel J.J. Estey of the Estey Organ Company in Brattleboro, Vermont. It was the first dormitory for women at a college.

The 1910 faculty of Shaw University on the front steps of Estey Hall. *State Archives of North Carolina.*

Shaw University Orchestra on the steps of Estey Hall, circa 1916. *Fundraising brochure for Estey Hall Foundation.*

Estey Hall, the first dormitory for women in the United States, served as the seminary on Shaw University campus. The students pictured are on various levels (1873–74). *State Archives of North Carolina.*

LEONARD MEDICAL, DENTAL, PHARMACY AND LAW SCHOOLS

Leonard Medical School was across the street from the campus to the west. In 1866, Dr. Tupper wanted to establish a medical school to train colored men to go as medical missionaries to Africa and work among their own people. In 1880, Judson Wade Leonard, Mrs. Tupper's brother, gave $5,000 toward the establishment of the medical school. In 1881, the General Assembly gave the land away as long as it was used for medical educational purposes. The first class entered in 1881, and the class of six graduated in 1886.

There was a four-year program for the medical school, the first of its kind in the country. By 1908, there were 301 graduates. The pharmacy school at that time had graduated 76. The school housed lecture rooms and dissecting rooms and had all appliances, including a number of costly models of human anatomy that were imported directly from Paris, France. It was considered one of the handsomest edifices in the South. The school was viewed with respect and admiration by whites.

Tyler Hall, built in 1910, was the site of the former hospital at Shaw University. *State Archives of North Carolina.*

There was limited hospital care available to members of the community. Those Blacks living in Raleigh received free medicine from the city, but non-residents had their board and medicine paid by their own counties.

Shaw also had a pharmacy and dental program. All of the medical programs were closed by 1918. Part of this was due to financial issues, some of which were brought on by the Flexner report created to centralize medical teaching across the country.

By 1883, a residential block had been created by the sale of land that had been the service yard of Governor Manly's mansion. Seventeen narrow lots were created for rental property from that land.

Shaw established a Law School, the first school of law for Blacks, in December 1888. The first graduating class was in 1890, and that graduate, Edward A. Johnson, was eventually made the dean of the law school, as well as being the principal of Washington School. When Johnson began to teach at the school, he not only taught the course on "Pleadings" but also taught shorthand and typewriting. The school saw these courses as an advantage to law students in finding positions in other firms that might not have openings for attorneys so that they might be more employable. By the time the school closed, in 1916, fifty-seven students had been graduated.

ENROLLMENT

SENIOR CLASS.

Name.	Postoffice Address.
Allen, William H.	Quitman, Ga.
DuBissette, Michael	Smithfield, N. C.
Edwards, Conrad A.	New York, N. Y.
Marks, J. E.	406 Bledsoe Ave., Raleigh, N. C.
McKenzie, B. G.	E. Tallahassee, Ala.
Robinson, Carodean R.	1031 Highland Ave., Winston, N. C.
Thomas, Edgar	338 Columbia St., Cambridge, Mass.

JUNIOR CLASS.

Cogdell, Annie Doris	67 Robeson St., Fayetteville, N. C.
McMurren, Noah	24 Tatems Lane, Elizabeth City, N. C.
Montgomery, Justine	36 President St., Charleston, S. C.

SOPHOMORE CLASS.

Baxter, Alice M.	35 Illinois Ave., Lake Forest, Ill.
Gilmer, Prather	726 E. Pettigrew St., Durham, N. C.
Gerran, Garland A.	High Point, N. C.
Graham, Dennis W.	Proctorville, N. C.
Rogers, Leroy	Raleigh, N. C.
Thompson, Elias B.	Lumberton, N. C.
Walker, Melvin D.	110 E. Leigh St., Richmond, Va.
Weddle, George W.	Denmark, Tenn.
Wimberly, Richard	Tarboro, N. C.
Wood, John R.	Hertford, N. C.

FRESHMAN CLASS.

Bowen, Fleetwood J.	East Hampton, Hampton, Va.
Armstrong, Elmo	Box 583, Rocky Mount, N. C.
Barrett, John	727 S. Person St., Raleigh, N. C.
Brown, Jessie	739 Fayetteville St., Raleigh, N. C.
Burgess, Thelma Virtue	527 S. East St., Raleigh, N. C.
Burt, Roger D.	Holly Springs, N. C.
Cartwright, Crosby	Bellcross, N. C.
Cheek, H. Y.	R. No. 1, Kittrell, N. C.
Clark, Minnie	120 W. South St., Raleigh, N. C.

GENERAL INFORMATION

THE SCHOOL YEAR

The next school year will begin Tuesday, October 1, 1918, and end May 31, 1919.

The dining-room will be open for supper Monday, September 30, 1918.

All new students in all departments, and all students who have failed to pass in any subject during the previous year, must register and report to their respective Deans for examination at 8:30, a. m., Wednesday, September 26.

On Thursday, September 27, all city students in all departments who are not required to take examinations on Wednesday will register.

On Friday, September 28, all former boarding students in all departments who are not required to take examinations on Wednesday will register.

DEPARTMENTS

There are the following departments: Industries, Music, Business, Academy, Teacher Training, College of Liberal Arts and Sciences, Schools of Theology, Pharmacy and Medicine.

EXPENSES

Important Notice

Annual incidental fee, payable on date of entrance	$ 3.00
Physical culture and athletic fee	1.00
Tuition, day students, payable in advance on the first day of each calendar month	1.50
Instrumental music (four lessons), payable in advance on the first day of each calendar month	1.75
Vocal music, same terms as instrumental	1.75
Board, room rent, tuition, heat, light, water and services of janitor, payable in advance, first day of each calendar month	12.50

Left: The 1917–18 Leonard Pharmacy School roster showing the author's grandfather Richard Wimberly before the school was closed. He finished at Meharry College in Tennessee. *DigitalNC, State Library of North Carolina.*

Right: Information page from the catalogue, circa 1915, after the Shaw Law School closed. *DigitalNC, State Library of North Carolina.*

LEONARD SCHOOL OF MEDICINE

CHARLES FRANCIS MESERVE, LL.D., *President.*

GEORGE H. STODDARD, A.M., *Dean.*

SAMUEL M. BECKFORD, M.D., *Professor of Anatomy, Associate in Physiology.*

........................, M.D., *Professor of Histology and Embryology and Demonstrator of Anatomy.*

GEORGE H. STODDARD, A.M., *Professor of Physiology, Associate in Pharmacology.*

PETER F. ROBERTS, M.D., *Professor of Pathology and Bacteriology.*

JOHN H. BIAS, A.B., *Professor of Chemistry.*

L. E. McCAULEY, M.D., *Professor of Pharmacology.*

LEMUEL T. DELANEY, M.D., *Professor of Surgery, Associate in Pathology.*

J. O. PLUMMER, M.D., *Professor of Physical Diagnosis and Hygiene.*

Left: Instructors at Leonard School of Medicine, from the catalogue after Charles Meserve became president of Shaw University. *DigitalNC, State Library of North Carolina.*

Free Dispensary.

A free dispensary is to be opened shortly in the Pharmacy Building at Shaw University. This will supply a long-felt want. At stated hours members of the medical faculty will be present and can be consulted by poor colored people who otherwise would be deprived of medical attendance. Medicines will be furnished when the patients are unable to purchase them. The opening of this free dispensary has been made possible by General Morgan, of New York, presenting to President Meserve his personal check of $100 for this purpose. It will be remembered that during the late war General Morgan commanded a brigade of colored troops. His interest in the colored race still survives in time of peace.

Left: The opening of a free dispensary for medicine at Shaw University. *From the* Gazette, *January 23, 1897.*

Below: Sanborn Fire Map showing Leonard Medical School and hospital building. *North Carolina Maps, State Archives of North Carolina.*

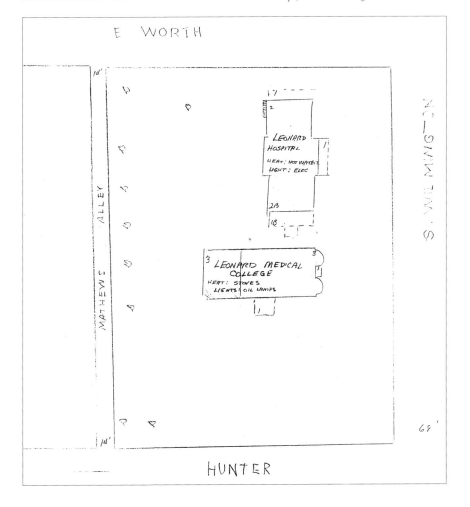

Program

Motto : Out of the Harbor

SUNDAY, MAY 9th, 1909

BACCALAUREATE SERMON . Rev. C. T. Walker, D. D., of Augusta

THURSDAY, MAY 13th
COMMENCEMENT DAY, 10 O'CLOCK A. M.

MUSIC

INVOCATION

MUSIC

ANNUAL ADDRESS . . . . . Hon. Elmer Ellsworth Brown
U. S. Commissioner of Education

MUSIC .

CONFERRING OF DEGREES . . . . . Frank M. Harper
Superintendent of City Schools, Raleigh, N. C.

ANNOUNCING OF PRIZES

AWARDING OF CERTIFICATES

PARTING ADDRESS TO GRADUATES President Charles Francis Meserve

MUSIC

BENEDICTION . . . . . . Rev. S. N. Vass, D. D.

This page: The 1909 commencement program for Leonard Medical and Pharmacy School at Shaw University. *Wake County Public Library, Olivia Raney Branch.*

Opposite: An aerial photo of Shaw University campus, circa 1960. Portions of the campus were sold to the City of Raleigh, 1964. *Wake County Public Library, Olivia Raney Branch.*

Shaw University Campus, circa 1960

Number	Name of Building
1	West Campus, Administration Building
2	West Campus, Student Center
3	West Campus, School of Religion
4	West Campus, Men's Residence Hall
5–11	Faculty homes (Faculty Row)
12	Portion of athletic practice field
13	Tyler Hall, University Library
14	Leonard Building
15	Home economics practice cottage
16	Faculty duplex
17	Meserve Hall, president's home
18	Science Hall
19	Estey Hall, women's dormitory
20	Shaw Hall
21	University Church

22	Spaulding Gymnasium
23	Tupper Hall, men's residence hall
24	Central heating plant
25	Convention Hall, men's residence hall and tennis court
26	Greenleaf Hall, university chapel and dining hall
27	Campus inn and bookstore
28	Garages
29	Maintenance shop
30	Raleigh Memorial Auditorium

DAVIE STREET PRESBYTERIAN CHURCH

In 1868, the Board of Church Expansion of the Presbyterian Church was approached about starting a Black church in Raleigh. Elder Godfrey Rainey and his wife from the Freedmen's Bureau visited to explore the idea. He found that the South wasn't ready to accept a church. His report recommended, instead, the establishment of a church school.

Rainey discussed this with Major George L. Lane, a local Black stonemason, civic leader and large landowner and developer, who obtained land to establish a mission at the southeast corner of Haywood and Davie Streets. The parochial school was opened at this location, and former slave children were taught there.

The Raineys and free-born African American H. Spencer were the first teachers in the school. They utilized the North Carolina education curriculum and added Bible studies, industrial education and music.

The parochial school was organized into a church. The original congregation purchased land and a plank building from the Raleigh Methodist Church at the corner of Davie and Person Streets and began regular services there in 1872. The original building was subsequently remodeled and enlarged by Calvin Lightner, a builder and eventual owner of Lightner Funeral Home and father of Raleigh's only Black mayor, Clarence Lightner.

TUPPER MEMORIAL BAPTIST CHURCH

In the fall of 1865, Dr. Henry M. Tupper met with "one-half dozen colored deacons and ministers" to teach them to learn to read and explain scripture at the Guion Hotel. His efforts were supported by the Freedmen's Bureau. His wife, Sarah, taught a class for women.

Advancing funds from his own pocket, Dr. Tupper purchased a small lot on the corner of Blount and Cabarrus Streets. There he began a school and then a church. Its first name was Second Baptist Church (Colored), and it was organized on February 17, 1866, with an original roll of twenty-two members—eighteen women and four men. The church's name was changed to Blount Street Baptist Church before becoming Tupper Memorial Baptist Church. It remains at its original site.

Part IV

POST–WORLD WAR II NEIGHBORHOODS/NATIONAL HISTORIC REGISTER

BATTERY HEIGHTS

Battery Heights was named because of the earthen batteries of the Civil War that were part of the fortification of the city of Raleigh ordered by Governor Zebulon Vance in 1863 to preserve the city of Raleigh in case of attack. The governor ordered slaves to build the fortification, and their owners were paid for the work. According to recent studies based on the maps of Lieutenant Colonel H.T. Guion, artillery and engineering, there is most likely still a battery formation in the original Battery Heights neighborhood between New Bern Avenue and Bart Street.

Bartholomew Gatling, father of John Gatling, bought a large amount of land in 1915. This land's boundaries were from Tarboro Road to Battery Drive and from New Bern Avenue to Davie Street. The land he purchased was divided into small lots and usually rented to Blacks who were moving out of the freedmen's villages.

John Gatling was considered a racist by those who lived in the neighborhood, according to a 1997 *News and Observer* article. As part of his estate, he created a scholarship at North Carolina State University for white men who had the name of Gatling or Gatlin. He grew up as a white southerner who watched his parents take shotguns and shoot over the heads of Black children who trespassed on their land.

There were fifteen acres behind the family home that John Gatling purchased during an intense inheritance lawsuit. In the early 1950s, Gatling recognized that he would have to sell the land to Black people. Due to

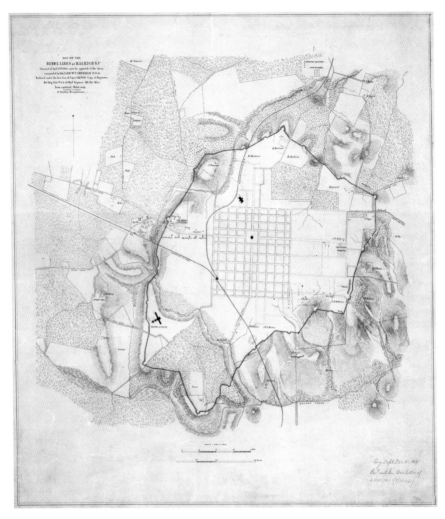

The 1865 Rebel line fortification map for the city of Raleigh during the Civil War. Battery Heights was named because of the battery formation located nearby. *City of Raleigh Museum.*

the growth of the Black communities, there was a color line (invisible but there nevertheless) that kept white people from buying property beyond the Gatling family house, and thus they would not move there. The land that the family home was situated on is now part of the City of Raleigh's Parks Department, and the park that sits on the land is called Roberts Park.

George C. Exum, a brick mason and teacher at Ligon High School, had done some work for John Gatling. Exum convinced Gatling to sell the property to Black professionals, and he was the one who recruited the families

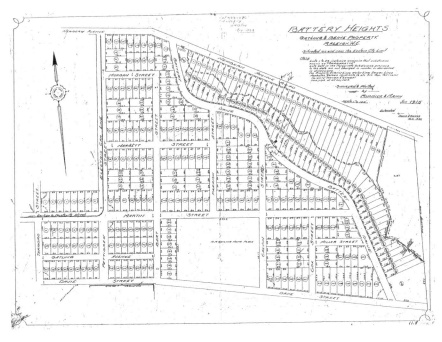

Above: Plat map for Battery Heights subdivision, 1915. *Wake County Register of Deeds.*

Left: The Gatling Street sign in Roberts Park neighborhood; the Gatling family owned the land in this area and in Battery Heights. *Author photo.*

to purchase the land. Before any piece of property was sold, Gatling had to meet individually with the person(s). Exum became the general contractor for the buildings and often hired his students to work on them.

According to Dr. George C. Debnam, Gatling wanted everybody who bought land to be on the same "moral, intellectual, and financial" level. The Debnams were the first family to move into Battery Heights in October 1959. Battery Heights was one of the first post–World War II subdivisions built for Black people. The larger neighborhood surrounding Roberts Park is also part of Battery Heights but not part of the National Historic Register.

The land that the houses were built on ranged from one-quarter to almost one acre. Most were in the one-third-acre size. Other requirements for the houses were setbacks of thirty feet from both the front and rear of the lots, as well as square footage of between twenty-five hundred and four thousand feet. Most of the area was forest and heavily wooded between the 1930s and 1940s. Many of the homes were designed by local designer and artist Jerry Miller, while others were chosen from Standard House plan books and had small alterations made.

1615 East Davie Street, Battery Heights, built circa 1959. *Author photo.*

300 Sherrybrook Drive, Battery Heights, built circa 1961. *Author photo.*

321 Sherrybrook Drive, home of the contractor and builder for most of the Battery Heights area, circa 1959. *Author photo.*

Raleigh Chapter of Old North State Medical, Dental and Pharmaceutical Society at the annual Christmas meeting in the basement of the home of Dr. Chris Hunt in Battery Heights. *Author family photo.*

The houses in Battery Heights were designed in a much more modern manner than those that were built during the same period in white subdivisions, which still used traditional designs with columns on the front, reminiscent of pre–Civil War styles. According to Jerry Miller, who designed homes in both the Battery Heights and Madonna Acres subdivisions, his clients often told him that they wanted their homes to look "different from everyone else's."

The neighbors became close friends and created a community association called Les Pins, which was suggested by Mrs. Elsie Perry, a French teacher, because of the tall pine trees in the neighborhood. Another nickname for the development by those who didn't live in the community was the "Gold Coast" because of the number of doctors living in the area. Notable residents in Battery Heights included:

- John Baker, the first Black sheriff elected in North Carolina since Reconstruction (1978), Oberlin Village native and a former NFL football player, and his wife, Juanita;

- Brad Thompson, former Raleigh city councilman and mayor pro-tem and state director for former U.S. Senator John Edwards; and Dorothy Thompson, former executive director of Project Enlightenment, a program of intervention for preschool children and their families;
- Cecil Goins, the second Black federal marshal in North Carolina and former Sergeant-at-Arms of the North Carolina Senate, and his wife, Laverne; and
- Dr. George C. Debnam (longtime Black physician) and Mrs. Marjorie Debnam (family and youth activist).
- Other medical professionals and their families included Dr. Chris Hunt, Dr. Robert McDowell and Dr. D.P. Lane.
- Teachers included William and Elsie Perry; Iris and Addie Lane; Dearl and Harriet Webster; Lawrence and Blanch Rivers; Vivian Lane; Margaret Lockamy; Norman, Lillian and Minnie McMillan; Charles and Daisy Robson; Dr. Frank and Anne Tolliver; James and Amelia Byers; William and Bernice Rainbow; and George and Marguerite Exum.

JOHN WINTERS

John Winters was born in 1920 in Raleigh to a family descended from free Blacks. His home was at the corner of Martin and East Streets. After moving to New York and attending several colleges, he returned to Raleigh to study at Shaw University. In 1941, he married, and together with his wife, Marie, he raised eight children. He worked at several different jobs to accomplish this but also built a home for himself and another family member during this period. Although he had jobs as a porter, waiter, delivery man and skycap, he began a real estate and insurance business, which became John W. Winters and Company. Before enlarging the business to include land development, he built some of the houses in Battery Heights. Upon construction of Madonna Acres subdivision, he enlarged the business to include land development.

Politically, in 1961, Winters became the first Black Raleigh city councilman since Reconstruction and then was appointed as a North Carolina senator from Wake County. He also served as a member of the North Carolina Utilities Commission and a member of the Board of Governors of the University of North Carolina system.

Jerry Miller, an artist and house designer, took the sketches drawn by Winters and created the final blueprints for construction of homes in Madonna Acres. He also designed some of the homes in Battery Heights.

Winters also developed the Biltmore Hills subdivision in southeast Raleigh. Built in 1962 for middle-class Black families, this area was greater than other subdivisions in physical size, but there were only four floor plans for buyers to choose from. They did not have the custom features or plans that the other subdivisions had, although owners made changes to their homes in later years.

ROCHESTER HEIGHTS

Rochester Heights is one and one-half miles southeast of downtown Raleigh. The boundary streets for Rochester Heights are Bailey Drive to the north, Boaz Road to the east, Calloway Drive to the south and Garner Road to the West.

Rochester Heights is a post–World War II National Historic Register designated subdivision in the Black Ethnic Heritage category. There was a need for much affordable housing after veterans returned from World War II. The city experienced quite a bit of growth after the war. Between 1945 and 1965, 18,256 buildings were constructed; 15,000 of those buildings were houses.

So many veterans were returning, and their families needed housing, so it had to be built quickly. There was no time for "brick by brick, detailed custom building.…[Things began to emerge] like standardized building modules, pre-hung doors, baseboards, and open spaces" for interiors, according to a *News and Observer* article written by Lori Roberts Wiggins in October 2010. Because of segregation and Jim Crow laws, few buildings were created for Black veterans or servicemen and their families. Not until the late 1950s were homes being constructed for Black families.

This subdivision was made up of thirty-nine acres that were sold to M.C. Garner on November 8, 1954. It was built between 1957 and 1964. The homes were all single-family, ranch-style homes. The lots varied in size from one-quarter to one-third of an acre.

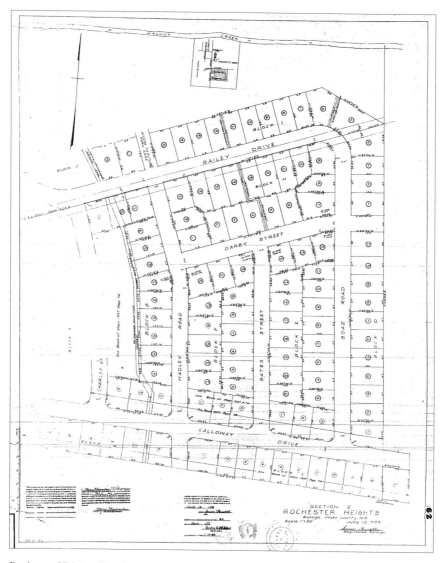

Rochester Heights #2, plat map showing Bailey Drive, Calloway Drive, Darby Street, Bates Street and Boaz Road. *Wake County Register of Deeds.*

The area had restrictive covenants that only allowed residential single-family detached dwellings. There were no Colonial-style homes built here. The restrictive covenants had setbacks of thirty feet from the street. No sidewalks were built before the Hadley Street/Calloway Drive crossing. The houses were not allowed to exceed two and a half stories in height, and there

1821 Charles Street, Rochester Heights, circa 1959. *Author photo.*

was an allowance for a private car garage with room for no more than two cars. The cost of each house could not be less than $6,000. The ground floor on two-story homes could not be less than eight hundred square feet.

The farmland that was purchased to build Rochester Heights originally belonged to Calvin Lightner, father of Mayor Clarence Lightner, the city's first Black mayor and an amazing citizen and entrepreneur in his own right. The farm extended from I-40 northeast to Rock Quarry Road and included Biltmore Hills and land farther into the city than Rochester Heights.

The streets in the subdivision were named for famous African Americans:

- Calloway Drive for Cab Calloway, singer and bandleader
- Bailey Street for Pearl Bailey, singer
- Charles Street for Ray Charles, singer and musician
- Doby Circle for Larry Doby, baseball player
- Bates Street for Clayton "Peg Leg" Bates, dancer with one wooden leg
- Waller Street for "Fats" Waller, jazz pianist, singer, composer and comedian

There are 137 contributing houses and outbuildings listed in the National Historic Register nomination packet. The neighborhood was developed from south to north. Calloway Drive was the first street to be completed

Above: Rochester Heights #1, plat map showing where it was built around Hillcrest Cemetery on Garner Road, on land originally owned by the Lightner family. *Wake County Register of Deeds.*

Opposite, top: Rochester Heights #3, plat map showing Charles Street and Calloway Drive. *Wake County Register of Deeds.*

Opposite, bottom: 721 Calloway Drive, home of the builder for most of the homes in Rochester Heights, circa 1957. *Author photo.*

and was the showpiece of the neighborhood. Phillips Building Corporation, owned by white developer E.E. Phillips, began issuing deeds in 1957. Key Homes took over after Phillips Building Corporation was no longer involved.

The designer and builders for the subdivision were Millard R. Peebles and his associates Sidney Cooley, Willis Hunter and Henry Neily. All of these men and their families lived in the neighborhood. Many of the families of the original owners still live in the neighborhood. Several of the original owners had been neighbors in Washington Terrace apartments before Rochester Heights was built.

801 Calloway Drive, home of one of the original brick masons in Rochester Heights, circa 1959. *Author photo.*

Rochester Heights had to be annexed to the city before the subdivision could be completed. The land that the Lightners sold was mostly woods, and it had to be cleared before any building could occur. Families would pick out the lot they wanted to purchase and choose which trees they wanted to be cleared.

Millard Peebles grew up in Oberlin Village, and his father was a masonry contractor. He became the builder for Rochester Heights. Peebles was the first Black person on the Raleigh Planning Commission. He came home from World War II, attended Hampton Institute in Hampton, Virginia, and received a building construction degree in the mid-'40s. He and his wife, Allie Muse Peebles, chose a lot on Calloway Drive and were the first family to move into the subdivision.

A *News and Observer* ad for Rochester Heights was titled, "A New Subdivision for Raleigh's Colored Families." The ad had a conceptual drawing of an open house plan that included a living room, kitchen, three bedrooms and a bath. The highlights in the ads were a modern three-bedroom brick home, no down payment to qualified buyers and payments of sixty dollars a month. The homes were sold by Cameron Brown Representatives. The ad also promised a limited-time free power lawn mower.

Another ad in the *News and Observer* was from G.S. Tucker and Brothers, Incorporated. It stated, "Rochester Heights Model Home Selects Norge Appliances." The pictures were of an eleven-cubic-foot Swing and Serve refrigerator freezer, a washer with a ten-pound tub and a Norge Deluxe thirty-six-inch range.

Information about the occupations of those who lived in the neighborhood includes the fact that thirty residents were either teachers or university professionals. Eight people worked with the United States Postal Service. Two were attorneys. Also included were pastors, janitors, mechanics, drivers, clerks, cooks, warehousemen and others. Several of the homeowners were Armed Forces veterans.

MADONNA ACRES

Madonna Acres is a thirteen-acre subdivision. It was the first subdivision created for Blacks by a Black developer with homes built to purchasers' specifications. The subdivision is to the east of St. Augustine's University. Delany Drive, the main street, runs from Glascock Street to Milburnie Road. There are three cul-de-sacs: Dillon Circle, Tierney Circle and Somerville Circle. There is another circle, but it is not listed in the National Historic Register.

The land was purchased by John Winters (the developer) from the heirs of Bishop Henry Delany of St. Augustine's College—the first black Suffragan bishop for Colored Work in North Carolina (charged with the responsibility of serving the church's Black population) and one of the first two Black bishops in any Episcopal diocese. (There were two bishops elected at the same time, but their consecration dates were not the same.) The subdivision was named for one of Winters's daughters, Donna.

Almost all of the houses were built between 1960 and 1965. All homes have a thirty-foot setback. There are twenty-four ranches, eleven split-levels, one split foyer and two two-story homes. The houses are brick with accent walls of stone veneer or wood. There is also a built-in planter and carport for every property. It is interesting to note that Clarence Coleman and J.D. Lewis co-purchased a third lot between their houses so that no one else could build on the property between them.

Of the thirty-eight original purchasers, twenty-eight worked in education, either in public school, higher education or the State Department of Public

Madonna Acres sign at the corner of Delany Drive and Milburnie Road. *Author photo.*

1505 Tierney Circle, built circa 1962. *Author photo.*

717 Delany Drive, built circa 1961. *Author photo.*

Instruction. These included George Stokes Jr. (Governor Morehead School); David and Leolia Spaugh; Richard Barfield (principal); Frank Weaver (State Department of Public Instruction); Igal Spraggins (registrar, St. Augustine's College); Rosalie Peay; Ocie and Dorothy Taylor; Ura H. Jones (Shaw University); Clinton R. Downing (education professor at East Carolina University); Hubert and Mary Poole; Francis and Wanda Poole; Christopher Gray (dean of men, St. Augustine's College); James Wilson; James Whitley; Sterling and Elaine Perry; Richard and Edwinton Ball (law professor, North Carolina Central University; educator, St. Augustine's College); P.U. Watson; Cora Lamb; Wetonah Williams; and Harold and Lucille Webb (State Department of Public Instruction/teacher).

Other owners' occupations included mortician, nurse, pharmacist, lab technician, janitor, kitchen staff, postal carrier, cab stand manager, beautician, freight handler, priest, upholsterer, photographer, tile mechanic and radio and TV announcer.

Many of the families who moved into Madonna Acres, Battery Heights or Rochester Heights had first lived in the Washington Terrace apartment complex. This was the first apartment complex built for Black professionals in Raleigh. It was built in 1951, and its first manager was Francis Poole, who also lived in Madonna Acres. Before Washington Terrace was built,

Left: Washington Terrace, the first apartment complex for African Americans (1951). Madonna Acres was eventually in the upper right. Oakwood Avenue is on the left, and St. Augustine's College is above left. *Aerial view, USDA Historical Maps, 1959.*

Below: 810 Delany Drive, built circa 1961. *Author photo.*

young middle-class Black couples and families didn't have apartments to lease. They either lived with family or rented available houses.

A number of the families who lived in Madonna Acres were prominent in fields other than education. Some of them included:

- Clarence and Marguerite Lightner. Clarence Lightner was the son of Calvin Lightner, a contractor and owner of Lightner Funeral Home. Clarence Lightner became a member of the Raleigh City Council and was elected as Raleigh's first and only (at this time) Black mayor in 1973. He also served as a Wake County senator, serving out the unexpired term of John Winters.

- Clarence and Ola Coleman. Clarence Coleman was a pharmacist and part owner of Hamlin Drugs on Hargett Street with Dr. John Johnson. Hamlin Drugs, started by James Hamlin, was the first registered pharmacy in the state of North Carolina. Mrs. Coleman was a lab technician at St. Augustine's College.
- J.D. and Louise Lewis. J.D. Lewis was an announcer for WRAL radio and then for WRAL TV. He was particularly famous for WRAL TV's Saturday Black dance show called *Teenage Frolics*. Their daughter Yvonne Lewis Holley, who was a state representative from Wake County, currently owns the house.
- Harold and Lucille Webb. Harold Webb was appointed the director of state personnel by Governor James B. Hunt Jr., the first Black person ever to serve in that position. He was also a Tuskegee airman. Mr. Webb served as a Wake County commissioner. Mrs. Webb was an educator before her retirement.

CONCLUSION

Raleigh's Black neighborhoods were created on the southeast side of the city in order to keep Black people from living where the white people lived. The size of the lots was noticeably smaller than those on the other side of town because they were originally created to be rental or leased lots and homes. The lots that were not between St. Augustine's College and Shaw University are usually larger than the lots around those areas because that was where Raleigh's Black middle class and more educated members of the population lived. Due to that education and increase in financial wealth, families were able to build homes that were more in keeping with the homes found in the white communities.

Today, as those smaller lots are purchased by people wanting to live closer to the downtown area, the houses are generally two stories in order to take advantage of all the space for building. There is very little yard left. Those families who purchased homes in the post–World War II neighborhoods have larger lots because they were designed and built as subdivisions. Trends are changing, and many of the houses that are in the National Historic Register neighborhoods are losing their character as they are modernized. The history behind their builds is important for all to know.

BIBLIOGRAPHY

Books

Carter, Dr. Wilmoth A. *Shaw's Universe: A Monument to Education Innovation.* Washington, D.C.: National Publishing, Inc., 1973.

———. *The Urban Negro in the South.* New York: Vantage Press, 1961. Repr., Forgotten Books, 2015.

Colored Race in America. Raleigh, NC: Edwards & Broughton Printing, 1900.

Corden, Robert. *The Negro in Reconstruction.* Englewood Cliffs, NJ: Prentice-Hall, Inc., 1969.

Crow, Jeffrey J., and Flora J. Hatley. *Black Americans in North Carolina and the South.* Chapel Hill: University of North Carolina Press, 1984.

Crow, Jeffrey J., Paul D. Escott and Flora I. Hatley Wadelington. *A History of African Americans in North Carolina.* N.p.: North Carolina Office of Archives and History, 2019.

Emory, Frank, ed. *Paths Towards Freedom: A Biographical History of Blacks and Indians in North Carolina by Blacks and Indians.* Raleigh: Center for Urban Affairs, North Carolina State University, 1976.

Federal Writers' Project. *Slave Narratives: A Folk History of Slavery in the United States from Interviews with Former Slaves.* Vol. 11. North Carolina Narrative, part 1, 1936–1938. N.p., n.d.

Foner, Eric. *Freedom's Lawmakers: A Directory of Black Officeholders during Reconstruction.* Baton Rouge: Louisiana State University Press, 1996.

Franklin, John Hope. *Reconstruction after the Civil War.* Chicago: University of Chicago Press, 1961.

Halliburton, Cecil D. *A History of St. Augustine's College, 1867–1937.* N.p., n.d.

Holaday, Chris, ed. *Baseball in the Carolinas: 25 Lessons on the State's Hardball Heritage.* Jefferson, NC: McFarland Publishers, 2002.

Johnson, K. Todd, and Elizabeth Reid Murray. *Wake: Capital County of North Carolina, Reconstruction to 1920,* Vol. 2. York, PA: Maple Vail Book Manufacturing Group, 2008.

Latta, Reverend Morgan L. *The History of My Life and Work: Autobiography of Reverend M.L. Latta.* Raleigh, NC: Edwards and Broughton Printing Press, 1903.

Logan, Frenise A. *The Negro in North Carolina, 1876–1894.* Chapel Hill: University of North Carolina Press, 1964.

Rabinowitz, Harold N. *Race Relations in the Urban South, 1865–1890.* Champaign: University of Illinois Press, 1980.

Raleigh Public Library. *20 Years: Richard B. Harrison Library.* Raleigh, NC: Irving-Swain Press, Inc., n.d.

Raleigh Sesquicentennial Commission. *Raleigh: Capital of North Carolina.* N.p., 1942.

Reid Murray, Elizabeth. *Wake: Capital County of North Carolina, Prehistory through Centennial.* Vol. 1. N.p.: Capital County Publishing Co., Inc., 1983.

Simmons-Henry, Linda. *The Heritage of Blacks in North Carolina.* Vol. 1. N.p.: N.C. African-American Heritage Foundation, Delmar Printing, 1990.

Simmons-Henry, Linda, and Linda Harris Edmisten. *Culture Town: Life in Raleigh's African American Communities.* Raleigh, NC: Raleigh Historic Districts Commission, Inc., 1993.

Trotter, Dr. Claude R. *History of the Wake Baptist Association, Its Auxiliaries and Churches, 1866–1966.* Raleigh, NC: Irving-Swain Press, 1990.

Unpublished Materials

Barbee, Mrs. J.M. "Historical Sketches of the Raleigh Public Schools, 1876–1941–1942." Barbee Pupils Association, 1943.

Barden, Albert Collection. Notes. State Archives of North Carolina.

The Bishop Tuttle School Report. St. Augustine's College. 1937–38.

Browning, George S. "The Services of the Richard B. Harrison Public Library, Raleigh, North Carolina." Unpublished thesis, 1962.

"The Clifton Conference: An Era of Progress and Promise." August 18–20, 1908.

"A Distinctive Contribution Commemorating the Bishop Tuttle Memorial Training School." St. Augustine's College, n.d.

First Congregational Church history. N.d.

Larson, Karl. "A Separate Reality: The Development of Racial Segregation in Raleigh, North Carolina, 1865–1915." Unpublished thesis, 1983.

Manly Street Christian Church annual. 1939.

Martin Street Baptist Church Centennial Celebration Book. N.d.

Mattson, Richard. "The Evolution of Raleigh's African-American Neighborhoods in the 19th and 20th Centuries." Unpublished thesis, 1988.

Morehouse, Henry Lyman. "H.M. Tupper, D.D.: A Narrative of Twenty-Five Years Work in the South, 1865–1890." N.d.

Raleigh Historic Districts Commission. New Bern Avenue/Edenton Street Historic Architectural Survey. Longleaf Historic Resources. City of Raleigh, 1998.

St. Augustine's College catalogue. 1915.
St. James AME Church history. N.d.
Tuttle Community Center. 1962 Progress Report. United Fund Agency Brochure.
Yeargin, J.W. "Facts Pertaining to Washington School." N.d.

National Register Historic Place Inventory, Nomination Forms

Battery Heights. rhdc.org/battery-heights-historic-district-0.
Berry O'Kelly Agriculture Building. rhdc.org/agricultural-building-berry-okelly-school.
East Raleigh/South Park. rhdc.org/east-raleigh-south-park-historic-district.
Madonna Acres. rhdc.org/madonna-acres-historic-district-2.
Oberlin Village. rhdc.org/oberlin-village-historic-district.
Rochester Heights. rhdc.org/rochester-heights-historic-district.
St. James AME Church. rhdc.org/saint-james-african-methodist-episcopal-church.
Tupper Memorial Baptist Church. rhdc.org/tupper-memorial-baptist-church.

City Directories

1880
1881
1884

Interviews

Burroughs, Mrs. Geraldine. Interview with author. Knightdale, North Carolina, October 18, 2021.
Camp, Dr. Norman. Interview with Jackie Turner. Raleigh, North Carolina, n.d.
Daniels, Lethia. Interview with Jackie Turner. Raleigh, North Carolina, n.d.
Holley, Yvonne Lewis. Interview with author. Raleigh, North Carolina, October 2021.
Joyner, Eunice. Interview with Jackie Turner. Raleigh, North Carolina, n.d.
Peebles-Brown, Elaine. Interview with author. Raleigh, North Carolina, November 11, 2021.

Culture Town *Interview Transcripts*

Beatty, Celestine. Interview with Lynn Hudson, 1988. raleighhrmprogram.catalogaccess.com/objects/9296.
Brown, Helen. Interview with Linda Simmons Henry, August 7, 1990. raleighhrmprogram.catalogaccess.com/objects/9279.
Dunbar, Louis, and Jesse Dunbar. Interview with Tim Tyson, September 7, 1988. raleighhrmprogram.catalogaccess.com/objects/9346.

Greene, Charlotte Haywood. Interview with Effie Williams, May 1989. raleighhrmprogram.catalogaccess.com/objects/9286.

Hamlin, Beatrice. Interview with Linda Simmons Henry, May 25, 1989.

Hamlin, Ernestine P. Interview with Terri Myers and Tim Tyson, April 10, 1988. raleighhrmprogram.catalogaccess.com/objects/9355.

Haywood, Julius. Interview with Linda Simmons Henry, June 6, 1989. raleighhrmprogram.catalogaccess.com/objects/9300.

Haywood, Norma. Interview with Loretta Hicks, May 22, 1989. raleighhrmprogram.catalogaccess.com/objects/9332.

Hodge, Rufus. Interview with Terri Myers, August 9, 1988. raleighhrmprogram.catalogaccess.com/objects/9347.

Hogan, Reverend Whalen. Interview with Grace P. Bethea, May 11–12, 1989. raleighhrmprogram.catalogaccess.com/objects/9315.

James, Mildred. Interview with Sharon Gibson, May 20, 1989. raleighhrmprogram.catalogaccess.com/objects/9351.

Lane, Dorothy. Interview with Terri Myers, May 4, 1989. raleighhrmprogram.catalogaccess.com/objects/9303.

Lightner, Clarence. Interview with Terri Myers, October 6, 1988. raleighhrmprogram.catalogaccess.com/objects/9334.

Ligon, Maye. Interview with Tim Tyson, July 12, 1988. raleighhrmprogram.catalogaccess.com/objects/9357.

Lockhart, Nora. Interview with Margaret Hayes, July 26, 1989. raleighhrmprogram.catalogaccess.com/objects/9282.

Pope, Joseph. Interview with Gertrude Pope, September 27, 1990. raleighhrmprogram.catalogaccess.com/objects/9307.

Pullen, Howard. Interview with Tim Tyson, August 9, 1988. raleighhrmprogram.catalogaccess.com/objects/9295.

Shaw, Angela Marchena. Interview with Terri Myers, September 9, 1988. raleighhrmprogram.catalogaccess.com/objects/9281.

Wall, Audrey. Interview with Loretta Hicks, May 22, 1989. raleighhrmprogram.catalogaccess.com/objects/9332.

Wilder, W.A. "Pete." Interview with Tim Tyson, May 22, 1989. raleighhrmprogram.catalogaccess.com/objects/9352.

Wilkins, Wilma Peebles. Interview with Terri Myers and Tim Tyson, July 11, 1988. raleighhrmprogram.catalogaccess.com/objects/9356.

Winters, John. Interview with Linda Simmons Henry, June 1, 1989. raleighhrmprogram.catalogaccess.com/objects/9314.

Newspapers

Briggs, Willis. *News and Observer*, August 8, 1948; October 20, 1935.

The Carolinian. "Hamlin Drugstore." February 10, 1977.

Daily Constitution, July 5, 1875.

Evening Visitor, June 15, 1891.

Gazette, April 10, 1897; July 31, 1897; January 23, 1897; "Training School for Nurses." July 24, 1897.

Hicks, Loretta. "Life During Segregation." *News and Observer*, December 29, 1991.

News and Observer, April 17, 1897; "Norma Haywood, Tarheel of the Week." June 3, 1990.

Raleigh Farmers and Mechanic, January 30, 1884.

Raleigh News, August 3, 1872; August 14, 1879.

Raleigh Times, October 31, 1907.

The Standard, September 7, 1869.

State Chronicle, May 26, 1887.

Sterling, Ben. "Reaching to Recapture Glory." *News and Observer*, February 8, 1997.

Weekly Era, February 26, 1874.

Yandle, C.E. "Community Waiting for State Help." *News and Observer*, April 11, 1988, 16C.

Magazines

Ben Chitty, Arthur. "St. Augustine College." *Historical Magazine for the Protestant Episcopal Church* 35, no. 3 (September 1966): 207–20. www.jstor.org/stable/42973155.

Cobb, Dr. W. Montague. "St. Agnes Hospital, Raleigh, North Carolina. 1896–1961." *Journal of the National Medical Association* 53, no. 5. (September 1961): 439–46.

Gay, Dorothy A. "Crisis of Identity: The Negro Community in Raleigh, 1890–1900." *North Carolina Historical Review* 150 (April 1973): 121–40.

Little, M. Ruth. "Getting the American Dream for Themselves." *North Carolina Historical Review* 98, no. 4 (n.d.).

Mitchell, Memory F. "The Good Works of St. John's Guild, 1877–1893." *North Carolina Historical Review* 63, no. 3 (July 1986): 314–15. www.jstor.org/stable/23518784.

Wool Parish, Katherine. "Rediscovering Lincolnville." *Our State*, October 2003, 104–6.

Maps

Insurance Maps of Raleigh. 1884, 1888, 1896, 1903, 1909. Sanborn Map Company, New York.

USDA Historical Aerial Maps, North Carolina State Archives.

Wake County Register of Deeds Historical Maps, land transfer maps (various).

Website Content

Documenting the American South. "Centennial Encyclopaedia of the African Methodist Episcopal Church Containing Principally the Biographies of the Men and Women, Both Ministers and Laymen, Whose Labors during a Hundred Years,

Helped Make the A.M.E. Church What It Is; Also Short Historical Sketches of Annual Conferences, Educational Institutions, General Departments, Missionary Societies of the A.M.E. Church, and General Information about African Methodism and the Christian Church in General; Being a Literary Contribution to the Celebration of the One Hundredth Anniversary of the Formation of the African Methodist Episcopal Church Denomination." docsouth.unc.edu/church/wright/wright.html.

Dowd, Jerome B. *Status of Prominent Living North Carolinians.* Raleigh: Edwards & Broughton, 1888. archive.org/details/sketchesofpromin00dowd/page/n1/mode/2up.

Ephesus Baptist Church History. "Our History." www.ephesusbaptistchurch.com/our-history.

Friends of Oberlin Village. "History of Oberlin Village." friendsofoberlinvillage.org.

Lincolnville AME Church. "History of Lincolnville AME Church." www.lincolnvilleamechurch.org/history.

National Archives. "The Freedmen's Bureau." archives.gov/research/african-americans/freedmens-bureau.

NC Consumer and Agriculture Department. "No State Fair." info.ncagr.gov/DeepFried/church-at-the-fair.

St. Ambrose. "Our History." stambroseraleigh.org/our-history.

St. Augustine's University. www.st-aug.edu/history.

Wilson Temple UMC Centennial History Book, 1871–1972. nccumc.org/history/wilso-temple-united-methodist-church-history.

Wilson Temple UMC Church History. wilsontempleumc.org/history.

INDEX

A

Aiken, M.W. 65
  Washington High School 63
American Baptist Home Mission
     Society of New York
  Shaw University 191
American Missionary Society 62, 124
American Missionary Society of NY
     61
Ames, Julia (Williams). *See* Williams,
     Julia A.
Anderson, Mr. and Mrs. Virgil 157
Anderson, W.H. 58
  Colored Educational Association of
     North Carolina 58
annexation 25, 27, 147, 220
Asbury 112
Atkins, Jim 155
Augustinus, Aurelius. *See* St.
     Augustine's College
Austin, Charity
  slave narratives 17
Avery, Reverend Charles 134

B

Bagley-Daniels-Pegues-Hamlin House
     183
Baker, John 212
  Oberlin 212
Baker, Juanita 212
Baker, Viney
  slave narratives 17
Barringer, Daniel 120
Barringer estate
  Raleigh Institute 121
baseball 72
  Bankhead, Dan 77
  barnstormers 76
  Chavis Park 76
  Covington, Wes 77
  Dove, Arthur 76
  Labor Day 75
  Neal, Charlie 77
  Shaw Alumni Field 75
  Shaw University 74
  Smith, Milt 77
  Smith, Pete 77
  Twilight League 74, 77
  Wilder, W.A. "Pete" 75, 76

baseball fields
  Lightner, Calvin 77
baseball teams 72
  Cincinnati Cardinals 77
  Delaware Potomacs 74
  Dodgers, LA 76
  House of David 76
  Raleigh Black Star Line 73
  Raleigh Cavs 76
  Raleigh Grays 73, 75, 76
  Raleigh Hard Sluggers 72
  Raleigh Swiftfeet 72
  Raleigh Tar Heels 73
  Raleigh Tigers 76, 77
  South Park Hornets 73, 74
Battery Heights
  Baker, John 212
  boundaries 207
  Civil War 207
  Debnam, Dr. George C. 210, 213
  freedmen's villages 207
  Gatling, Bartholomew 207
  Gatling, John 207
  Goins, Cecil 213
  Guion, Lieutenant Colonel H.T. 207
  Hunt, Dr. Chris 213
  Lane, Dr. D.P. 213
  McDowell, Dr. Robert 213
  Miller, Jerry 210, 212
  nicknames 212
  South Park/East Raleigh 174
  Thompson, Brad 213
  Washington Terrace 224
  Winters, John 213
Battle, Dr. Kemp P. 134, 139
Benson, May 139
Berry O'Kelly Training School 105, 109
  Agriculture Building 108
  Rosenwald Foundation 108
Best, R.W. 49
Biltmore Hills 214
  Lightner, Calvin 181
Bishop Tuttle Memorial Training
    School 131, 143. *See also* St.
    Augustine's College

Brotherhood of St. Andrew 145
  Christian social service 143
  Community Chest Agency 144
  Fisher Farm 145
  Hunter, Reverend and Mrs. A.B. 143
  Hunter, Sarah 143
  Penny Savings Bank 144
  programs 144
  St. Agnes Training School for Nurses
      145
  St. Augustine's College 143
  United Way 144
Bledsoe, Moses 120, 176
boardinghouses 179
  Harris boardinghouse 179
  Lewis Hotel 179
  Smoky Hollow 179
  Starksvilla Guest House 179
books
  *Baseball in the Carolinas: 25 Lessons on the
      States' Hardball Heritage* 74
  Culture Town 35, 62
  Lunsford Lane, autobiography 21
Boy Scouts 125
Branch, Professor John 62
Brewer, Adele 62
Brewer, Reverend Fisk P. 61, 62, 124
  First Congregational Church 61
  Washington Graded School 61, 120
Brody, G.W. 51
Brooklyn
  boundaries 118
  Shaffer map 118
Brooks, Amos 126
Broughton, Needham B. 56
Browning, Aaron "Sink" 74
Bucket and Ladder Company 71
  Butler, J.W. 71
  Gorham, A.L. 71
  Johnston, Ephraim 71
  Lane, G.E. 71
  Winston, J.W. 71
Buncombe, H.P.
  Victor Fire Company 69
Burgess, Marie 141

Burns, Tony 161
business 33
  barbershops 34, 48
  City Market 35
  entrepreneur 34
  Fayetteville Street 33
  Hargett Street 33, 36
  Lane, Lunsford 18
  railroad 18
  restaurants 34
  slaves 18
Butler, J.W. 71

C

Cameron Estate 99
Camp Ellis
  Ellis, Governor John W. 134
Camp Russell
  Camp Ellis 134. *See also* St.
    Augustine's College
Cannon Lands 119
  boundaries 119
  railroads 119
Capehart, Dr. Lovelace 180
  Washington Graded School 62
Capitol
  Lane, Major George L. 164
  Williams, Tom 164
Carnage, Fred J. 147
Carrington, Sarah
  Lincolnville AME Church 116
Carter, Dr. Wilmoth
  Shaw's Universe 194
Caswell, John P. 58
  Colored Educational Association of
    North Carolina 58
  Wake County commissioner 120
Caswell, John R. 120
cemeteries 93, 105, 116, 136, 144, 181
  Method 106
Centennial Graded School 54, 56, 182
Chavis Heights 67, 79
  South Park/East Raleigh 174
  Works Progress Administration 79

Chavis Park 76
  Bickett, attorney William Y. 78
  Daniel, Paul A. 78
  General Assembly 78
  Knapp, Jack 79
  National Recreation Association 79
  Weathers, Curtis A. 78
  Wilder, W.A. "Pete" 79
  Works Progress Administration 79
  Young, Mrs. Hubert 78
Chavis School, the 60, 183
Christ Church
  St. Augustine's College 134
Christ Episcopal Church 152
  St. Paul AME Church 152
churches 30, 97, 142, 151
  Davie Street Presbyterian Church
    125, 164, 179, 202
  Ephesus Baptist Church 113
  Fayetteville Street Baptist Church
    124
  First Baptist Church 155
  First Baptist Church of Oberlin 101
  First Colored Baptist Church 156
  First Congregational Church 124
  First Cosmopolitan Baptist Church
    124
  Hall's Chapel 101
  Lincolnville AME Church 113
  Macedonia New Life Church 123
  Manly Street Christian Church 123
  Martin Street Baptist Church 157
  Mount Moriah Baptist Church 101
  Neville's Episcopal Church 127
  Oak City Baptist Church 106
  Oberlin Baptist Church 101
  Rush Metropolitan Church 178
  Second Baptist Church 25
  St. Ambrose Episcopal Church 102,
    154, 155
  St. Augustine Episcopal Church 151
  St. James AME Church 106
  St. Paul AME Church 57, 151, 152
  Tupper Memorial Baptist Church 26

Church of the Good Shepherd
   Rick, Reverend Edward Robbins 143
City Market 105
   Victor Fire Company 71
City of Raleigh 120, 125
   Harris, James H. 102
Civil War 17, 25, 26, 52, 94, 119, 123,
      163, 174, 178
   Battery Heights 207
   Confederate surrender 192
Clark, Ella 131
Coleman, Clarence 226
   Hamlin Drug Company 226
   pharmacist 226
Coleman, Ola 226
College Park
   boundaries 146
   Carnage, Fred J. 147
   Fisher Farm 146
   Fort, D.J., Jr. 146
   Lincoln Park 146
   occupations 147
   St. Augustine's College 147
   water and sewer lines 147
Collins, I.R. 139
Colored Educational Association of
      North Carolina
   General Assembly 58
Confederate Old Soldiers' Home 77
Constitution, North Carolina 142
   education 54
Cooke, Reverend William D.
   Lincolnville AME Church 116
Cotton, John W. 129
   Idlewild Plantation 129
   North Carolina Land Company 129
Cotton Place 48, 157, 163
   boundaries 129
   Hunter, Charles N. 129
   Idlewild Plantation 129
   Raleigh Cooperative Land and
         Building Association 129
   South Park/East Raleigh 174
Cox, General William 134

Cox Memorial Church 127
Cozart, L.S.
   Washington High School 63
Crawford, William R. 112
Crosby-Garfield School 59, 60
   Ligon, John W. 111
   Watson's Addition 60
Crosby, Henry 60
Crosby School 57, 171
   Williams, Julia A. 60
Crosby, W.L. 59
Crossan, Robert 161
   Police 24
Culture Town 62, 103, 105, 116
   James, Mildred 133
   Pullen, Howard 72, 131

D

Daniels, Josephus 183
Davie Street Parochial School
   Lane, Major George L. 164
Davie Street Presbyterian Church 164,
      202
   Davie Street Parochial School 202
   Lane, Major George L. 164, 202
   Lightner, Calvin 179, 202
   Raleigh Methodist Church 202
   Spencer, H. 202
Davis, Confederate president Jefferson
   Jones, James H. 69
Davis, Reverend Alfred 62
DeBerry, Reverend Perfect R. 125
Debnam, Dr. George C. 210, 213
Debnam, Marjorie 213
Delany, Bishop Henry 137, 139
Delany, Dr. Lemuel 131, 139
   St. Agnes Training School for Nurses
      131
Delaware Potomacs
   Browning, Aaron "Sink" 74
   Johnson, William "Judy" 74
Depression 181
Devane, Dr. Carl 148
Deweese, J.J. 51

doctors
  Battle, Dr. Kemp P. 139
  Capehart, Dr. Lovelace 62, 180
  Debnam, Dr. George C. 213
  Delany, Dr. Lemuel 131, 139
  Duncan, Dr. Jenny A. 141
  Glendon, Dr. Mary P. 141
  Hayden, Dr. Catherine P. 141
  Haywood, Dr. Richard 161
  Hunt, Dr. Chris 213
  Knox, Dr. Augustus 139
  Lane, Lunsford 21
  Lewis, Dr. Richard H. 139
  McDowell, Dr. Robert 213
  McKee, Dr. James 139
  Pope, Dr. Manassa 180, 182, 183
  Royster, Dr. Hubert 139
  Royster, Dr. W.I. 139
  Scruggs, Dr. Lawson A. 139
Dove, Arthur 76
Dunbar, Jesse 149
Dunbar, Louis 62, 149
  Washington Graded School 62
Duncan, Dr. Jenny A. 141
Dunn, Adline Virginia 163
Dunston, B.H. 122
Dunston, Sylvester
  Victor Fire Company 69

E

East Raleigh
  boundaries 178
  Calvin Lightner 179
  Civil War 178
  Old Fairgrounds 178
  Richard B. Harrison Library 178
  Rush Metropolitan Church 178
East Raleigh School 59
Edenton Street Church 152
  St. Paul AME Church 152
education 54, 56, 107
  Centennial Graded School 54, 56
  Chavis School, the 60
  Colored Women's Association 57

  Crosby School 57
  Episcopal Parish School 58
  First Congregational Church 125
  Freedmen's Aid Society of
      Pennsylvania 57
  Freedmen's Bureau 58, 62
  Garfield School 56, 57
  General Assembly 58
  Howell, Superintendent Logan D. 57
  Institute for Deaf, Dumb and Blind
      26
  James, Mildred 57
  Johnson School, the 56, 57, 151
  Latta University 97, 99
  Lucille Hunter School 60
  McAlpine, Superintendent Andrew
      J. 56
  Miles School, the 58
  Moses, Edward P. 56
  nursery school 125
  Oberlin School 56, 97
  Raleigh Institute 26
  Rosenwald Foundation 107
  Shaw University 26, 57
  St. Ambrose Episcopal Church 58
  St. Augustine's College 57
  trade school 125
  Tuskegee Conference 107
  Washington Graded School 56, 61
educators and teachers 79, 213
  Brewer, Adele 62
  Crosby, Henry 60
  Crosby, W.L. 59
  Freedmen's Aid Society of
      Pennsylvania 57
  Friends Freedmen's Aid Society 58
  Graves, Anne Fannie 57
  Harris, James H. 101
  Hayes, Esther P. 61
  Hunter, Charles N. 59
  Hunter, Lucille 61
  Jeffries, Louise 60
  Ligon, John W. 111
  Oberlin School 98

O'Hara, J.E. 58
Paisley, J.W. 60
Warwick, Louisa 58
Warwick, Reverend W.M. 58
Williams, Julia A. 98
Edwards, Reverend Thomas 160
Ellis, Governor John W. 134
entertainment 35
entrepreneurs
Lane, Major George L. 161, 164
Lightner, Calvin 179
O'Kelly, Berry 35, 106, 109
Yeargin, J.W. 64
Ephesus Baptist Church 113, 116, 117
Episcopal Parish School
Freedmen's Bureau 58
Estey, Colonel J.J.
Estey Organ Company 194
Estey Hall 194
Exum, George C. 208
brick mason 208
educator 208

F

Fayetteville State University 179
fire companies
Bucket and Ladder Company 71
Fire Company No. 1 69
Phoenix Chemical Company 71
Victor Fire Company 69
First Baptist Church 151, 155
Atkins, Jim 155
Baptist Grove 155
dismissal of members 155
education 58
First Colored Baptist Church 156
Jett, Henry 155
Jones, Willie 155
Moore Square 155
Roman Catholic Church of St. John
the Baptist 156
Smoky Hollow 156
state house 155
Warrick, Reverend W.M. 156

First Baptist Church of Oberlin 101
First Colored Baptist Church 156
First Congregational Church 61, 124
American Missionary Society 124,
125
Boy Scout troop 125
Brewer, Reverend Fisk P. 124
City of Raleigh 125
Community United Church of Christ
125
Cunningham, Reverend Howard 125
Davie Street Presbyterian Church
125
DeBerry, Reverend Perfect R. 125
Fourth Ward 124
Freedmen's School 124
Mott, Reverend J.J. 124
nursery school 125
Pullen Memorial Baptist 125
Smith, Reverend George 125
trade school 125
urban renewal 125
Washington Graded School 61, 124
First Cosmopolitan Baptist Church
123
Fayetteville Street Baptist Church
124
Fayetteville Street Little Mission
Church 123
Little Mission Church 123
urban renewal 124
Fort, D.J., Jr. 146
Fourth Ward 123, 124
Hayti 119
Raleigh City Urban Renewal and
Planning Commission 120
Freedmen's Aid Society of Pennsylvania
57
Freedmen's Bureau 17, 23, 51, 52, 53,
54, 58, 134, 192
Educational Department 53
Howard, General O.O. 23, 52
Miles, General Nelson A. 58
Riddick, Private Samuel 52

Vogel, Dr. H.C. 53
Freedmen's Convention 101, 152
freedmen's villages 29, 129
  Cannon Lands 29
  Cotton Place 29, 129
  Hayti 29
  Hungry Neck 29
  Idlewild 29, 129, 130
  Manly's Homestead 29
  Old Fairgrounds 29
  Smith-Haywood 29
  St. Petersburg 29
  Wilmington-Blount 29

G

Garfield School 56, 57, 59, 60
  Crosby, W.L. 59
  Ligon, John W. 60
Garrison, William Lloyd 21
Garvey, Marcus 73
Gatling, John 29, 157, 207
  Exum, George C. 208
  North Carolina State University 207
General Assembly 196
  charters 58, 69, 71
  College Park 147
  House of Representatives 102
  Lincoln Park 147
  Little, George 50
  private laws 69, 123
  resolutions 49
  Senate 102, 213
  session laws and acts 20, 78, 154, 155
Glendon, Dr. Mary P. 141
Goins, Cecil 213
  federal marshal 213
  Senate, sergeant-at-arms 213
Goins, Laverne 213
Gorham, A.L. 71
Governor's Palace 61, 120, 123
Grant, President Ulysses 102
Groom, M.G.
  Wilson Temple UMC 100
Guion Hotel 203

Gurley, Milford
  Fourth Ward 171

H

Hall, Reverend Plummer T. 101
Hall's Chapel 101
Hamlin, Dr. Tom 184
  Community Drug Store (Raleigh,
    NC) 184
  Community Drug Store (WV) 184
  Howard University 184
  Leonard School of Pharmacy 184
Hamlin Drug Company 184
  Coleman, Clarence 226
  Hamlin, James 226
  Johnson, Dr. John 226
Hamlin, Ernestine P. 194
  Centennial Graded School 182
  Chavis School, the 183
  Estey Hall 183
  Hamlin, Dr. Tom 184
  Institute for Deaf, Dumb and Blind
    184
  Kay, Willie Otey 183
  Paige 183
  Pegues, Dr. Albert Witherspoon 182
  Pope, Dr. Manassa 182
  Shaw University 183, 184
  Taylor, Mildred Otey 183
  Washington Graded School 183
  Wheeler, Martha 183
Hampton Institute 179, 220
  trade school 138
Hargett Street 32, 33, 51, 66, 71
  Community Drug Store 184
  Hamlin Drug Company 184
Harris, James H. 48, 95, 101
  City of Raleigh 102
  Colored Educational Association of
    North Carolina 58
  Congress 102
  educator 101
  Freedmen's Convention 101
  Grant, President Ulysses 102

Institute for Deaf, Dumb and Blind 102
National Convention of Colored Men 101
New England Freedmen's Aid Society 101
North Carolina House of Representatives 102
North Carolina Republican 102
North Carolina Senate 102
Oberlin College 101
Oberlin Village 96
presidential elector 102
Raleigh Gazette 102
Republican 102
St. Ambrose Episcopal Church 102
travels 101
Twenty-Eighth Regiment of Colored Troops 101
Harrison, Richard B. 66
Harris, W.N. 163
Hayden, Dr. Catherine P. 141
Hayes, Esther P. 61
Hayes, Washington 137
Hayti 120, 122
Fourth Ward 119
occupations 120
Raleigh Cooperative Land and Building Association 120
Southside 119
urban renewal 120
Haywood, Barbara 57
Johnson School, the 57
Haywood, Charles A. "Doll" 73
Haywood, Dr. Richard 161
Haywood, William H. 137
Hillcrest Cemetery 181
Hodge, Reuben 161
Hodge, Rufus
City Market 35
Hogan, Reverend Whalen 103, 105
Holden, Governor William W. 23, 51
Holland, Anna W. 64
Holley, Yvonne Lewis 226

Howard, General O.O. 23, 52
Howard University 116, 184
Howell, Superintendent Logan D. 57
Hungry Neck 48, 126
boundaries 126
Brooks, Amos 48, 126
business 127
Cox Memorial Church 127
Democrats 127
Neville's Episcopal Church 127
Raleigh Cooperative Land and Building Association 126
Rhone, Oliver 127
Second Ward 127
Union Billiard Hall and Saloon 127
YMCA 127
Hunt, Dr. Chris 213
Hunter, Charles M.
Victor Fire Company 69
Hunter, Charles N. 59
Hunter, Charlie H. 57
Graves, Anne Fannie 57
Johnson School, the 57
St. Paul AME Church 57
Hunter, Lucille
educator 61
Hunter, Reverend Aaron 138
Bishop Tuttle Memorial Training School 143
St. Augustine's College 138
trade school 138
Hunter, Sarah 138, 139, 144
St. Agnes Training School for Nurses 139
St. Augustine's College 138

I

Idlewild 48, 130, 131
ballpark 131
boundaries 130
Clark, Ella 131
Oakwood 131
Pullen, Howard 131
Idlewild Plantation 129

Institute for Deaf, Dumb and Blind 26, 29, 62, 102, 178, 182, 184
Iseley, Mayor George 66

J

James, Mildred 133
  First Baptist Church 133
  Idlewild 133
  Seaboard Railroad 133
Jefferson, President Thomas 135
Jeffries, Louise 60
Jett, Henry 155
Johnson, E.A.
  attorney 171
  dean of law school 197
  developer 171
  Richard B. Harrison Library 68
  Shaw University 171
  South Park 176
  Washington Graded School 62, 171
Johnson School, the 56, 151, 152
  Graves, Anne Fannie 57
Johnston, Ephraim 71
Jones, H.C.
  Victor Fire Company 69
Jones, James H. 69
  police and sheriff 69
  Victor Fire Company 69
Jones, Katie 116
Jones, Moses 116
  Ephesus Baptist Church 116
Jones, Willie 135, 155
  Jefferson, Thomas 135
Jordan, Reverend Patrick James
  Lincolnville AME Church 116

K

Kay, Willie Otey 183
Kingsland, Richard 49
Kittrell College 116
Knox, Dr. Augustus 139
Ku Klux Klan 141

L

land companies 48
  National Freedmen's Savings and
    Trust Company 48, 51, 94
  North Carolina Land Company 48,
    94
  Raleigh Cooperative Land and
    Building Association 48, 94
  Raleigh Land and Improvement
    Company 48, 50
  Union Enterprise Company 48
Lane, Allen 163
Lane, Charles
  Lincoln University 164
  Shaw University 164
Lane, Dr. D.P. 213
Lane, G.E. 71
Lane, George
  Lincoln University 164
  Shaw University 164
  state bar exam 164
Lane, Lunsford 19
  autobiography 21
  Curtis, Martha 20
  Dudley, Governor Edward B. 20
  entrepreneur 19
  family 19
  freedom 20
  Lane, Joel 19
  physician 21
  Senate 20
  Smith, Benjamin B. 20
Lane, Major George L. 161
  Davie Street Parochial School 164
  Davie Street Presbyterian Church
    164
  developer 164
  Dunn, Adline Virginia 163
  entrepreneur 164
  furniture maker 164
  general store 164
  Lane, Charles 164
  Lane, George 164
  Lane's Bottom 161, 164

quarry freedmen 164
  undertaker 164
Lane's Bottom 164
Lassiter meal 105
Latta, Reverend Morgan L. 97, 99
  autobiography 99
  Latta University 99
  Shaw University 99
Latta University 97, 99
Lee, Mollie Huston 66, 68
Lee, Sheriff Timothy F. 94, 95
Leonard School of Medicine 183
  graduates 196
  Scruggs, Dr. Lawson A. 139
Leonard Schools of Medicine,
      Pharmacy, Dental and Law
  Leonard, Judson Wade 196
Levister, Professor J.L. 62
  Washington High School 63
Lewis, Dr. Richard H. 139
Lewis, J.D. 226
  Holley, Yvonne Lewis 226
  Teenage Frolics 226
  WRAL TV 226
Lewis, Louise 226
library
  Iseley, Mayor George 66
  Library Commission of North
    Carolina 66
  North Carolina Department of Public
    Instruction 66
  Richard B. Harrison Library 66
Library Commission of North Carolina
  67
Lightner Arcade 179
  Basie, Count 179
  Calloway, Cab 179
  Ellington, Duke 179
  Hargett Street 179
Lightner, Calvin 77, 217, 220
  Biltmore Hills 181
  Brown Funeral Home 179
  city commissioner 180
  construction 179

  Davie Street Presbyterian Church
    179
  Depression 181
  farm 181
  funeral home 179, 180
  Hillcrest Cemetery 181
  Lightner Arcade 179
  Lightner Building 179
  Lightner, Clarence 179, 202
  Lightner Funeral Home 202
  Mechanics and Farmers Bank 179
  Pope, Dr. Manassa 180
  Rochester Heights 181, 217
  Seneca, Bob 180
  Shaw University 179
Lightner, Clarence 179, 181, 202, 217,
  225
  Lightner, Calvin 179, 225
  Lightner Funeral Home 225
  mayor of Raleigh 217, 225
  Raleigh City Council 225
  senator 225
Lightner, Marguerite 225
Ligon High School 208
Ligon, John W. 60
  City of Raleigh politics 111
  Crosby-Garfield School 111
  education 111
  Garfield School 60
  home 111
  Method 110
  Shaw University 110
  Tupper Memorial Baptist Church
    110
  Union Reformer 111
Lincoln Day School
  Friends Freedmen's Aid Society 58
  Guion Hotel 58
  Lincoln Sunday School 58
  New England Freedmen's
    Commission 58
Lincoln Park
  Carnage, Fred J. 147
  water and sewer lines 147

Lincoln, President Abraham 17, 23
Lincoln University 164
Lincolnville 29, 112
  Asbury 112
  Carter-Finley Stadium 112
  Crawford, William R. 112
  Ephesus Baptist Church 113
  flooding 113
  freedmen's villages 112
  nicknames 112
  North Carolina Agricultural
    Association 112
  North Carolina State University 112
  unsanitary conditions 112
Lincolnville AME Church 113, 116,
  117
  building purchase 117
  Carrington, Sarah 116
  Carter-Finley Stadium 116
  Ephesus Baptist Church 116
  Jones, Moses 116
  North Carolina State University 116
  pastors 116
  Village of Yesteryear 117
Little, George 48
Lockhart, Hardy 152
  Colored Educational Association of
    North Carolina 58
Long, Alex 58
  Colored Educational Association of
    North Carolina 58
Lucille Hunter School 60

M

Macedonia New Life Church 123
  Baptist Grove 123
  Fourth Ward 123
  General Assembly 123
  Governor's Palace 123
  Manly Street Christian Church 123
  Manly Street United Church of
    Christ 123
  Moore Square 123
  urban renewal 123

Watts Chapel 123
Madonna Acres
  boundaries 222
  Delany, Bishop Henry 222
  educators 222
  Miller, Jerry 214
  occupations 224
  Poole, Francis 224
  St. Augustine's College 222
  Washington Terrace 224
  Winters, John 222
Manly, Governor Charles 120, 122,
  128
Manly's Homestead
  Barringer, Daniel 120
  Barringer estate 121
  Bledsoe, Moses 120
  Manly, Governor Charles 120
Marshall, Henry 163
Martin Street Baptist Church 157
  Anderson, Mr. and Mrs. Virgil 157
  Edwards, Reverend Thomas 160
  Wimberley, Reverend Elias 160
Mason, Lewis 103
Mason, Reverend Richard S.
  Christ Church 134
Matthews, W.H. 58
  Colored Educational Association of
    North Carolina 58
McAlpine, Superintendent Andrew J.
  56
McDowell, Dr. Robert 213
McKee, Dr. James 139
Mechanics and Farmers Bank
  Lightner, Calvin 179
Memorial Auditorium 120, 123
Method 29
  Berry O'Kelly Training School 106
  boundaries 103
  businesses 105, 108
  cemetery 105
  Cox, General W.R. 103
  Hogan, Reverend Whalen 103
  Mason, Lewis 103

nicknames 103, 105
North Carolina State University 105
Oak City Baptist Church 106
occupations 103
O'Kelly, Berry 108
O'Kelly, Isaac 103
post office 106, 109
property owners, first 103
Raleigh Township School 105
schools 105, 106
Southern Railroad Company 106
St. James AME Church 106
Wood, C.H. 108
Miller, Jerry 210, 212
Battery Heights 212, 214
Madonna Acres 212, 214
missionaries
education 54
Mitchell, W.B.
Victor Fire Company 69
Morgan, W.H. 95
Morgan, Wilson 58
Colored Educational Association of
North Carolina 58
Wilson Temple UMC 100
Moses, Edward P. 56
Mother Bethel Church 116
Mott, Reverend J.J. 124
Mount Moriah Baptist Church 101

N

National Freedmen's Savings and Trust
Company 48, 94
Brody, G.W. 51
Deweese, J.J. 51
Harris, James H. 51
Holden, Governor William W. 51
Pulliam, R.W. 51
Swepson, George 51
National Negro Business League 110
Nazareth 29
Neville's Episcopal Church 127
New England Freedmen's Aid Society
101, 191

Shaw University 191
newspapers 33, 72
News and Observer 96, 133
North Carolina Republican 102
Raleigh Gazette 102
Raleigh Independent 109
Union Reformer 111
Norfolk Southern Railway 148
North Carolina Agricultural
Association 157
North Carolina Land Company 48,
94, 129
Best, R.W. 49
Cotton Place 49
freedmen 49
Kingsland, Richard 49
Little, George 48
Oberlin 49
Swepson, George 48
North Carolina State University 112,
207
Lincolnville 112
Washington High School 64

O

Oak City Baptist Church 106
Oberlin 29, 48
Oberlin Baptist Church 101
Oberlin College 96
Harris, James H. 96
Oberlin, Jean Frederick 96
Oberlin, Jean Frederick 96
Oberlin School 56, 97, 98
O'Kelley, Nanny 98
Peace, Fannie 98
Richardson, Kittie 98
Williams, Julia A. 98
Oberlin Village 94, 95, 96, 97, 100,
118, 220
annexation 100
Cameron, Paul 93
churches 97
Depression 100
Harris, James H. 95

Latta University 97, 99
Lee, Sheriff Timothy F. 94, 95
Morgan, W.H. 95
National Freedmen's Savings and
    Trust Company 94
News and Observer 96
nicknames 96
North Carolina Land Company 94
Oberlin, Jean Frederick 96
Peck, Lewis W. 93, 95
Pettiford, Jesse 93
Raleigh Cooperative Land and
    Building Association 94, 95
San Domingo 95
Smith, Dr. Albert 95
Turner, John 97
Williams, Thomas 93
occupations 21, 119, 120, 128, 139,
    148, 163
hostler 120
O'Hara, J.E. 58
Colored Educational Association of
    North Carolina 58
O'Kelley, Nanny 98
O'Kelly, Berry 105, 106
Berry O'Kelly Training School 109
business 106
entrepreneur 35, 109
Kittrell College 110
Mechanics and Farmers Bank 109
National Negro Business League 110
postmaster 106, 109
Raleigh Independent 109
Rosenwald, Julius 107
store 108
Turner, John 109
Tuskegee Conference 107
Western Wake Highway 110
O'Kelly, Isaac 103
Old Fairgrounds 72, 77, 129
Gatling, John 157
North Carolina Agricultural
    Association 157
Parker, M.A. 157

Stronach, W.C. 157
Otey family
barber 34
Kay, Willie Otey 34

P

Page, Jimmy 149
Paige car 183
Paisley, J.W. 60
Parker, M.A. 157
pastors
Warwick, Reverend W.M. 58
Patterson, Moses 58
Colored Educational Association of
    North Carolina 58
Peace, Fannie 98
Peace Institute 192
Peck, Lewis W. 93, 95
Peebles, Allie Muse 220
Peebles, Millard 218, 220
Hampton Institute 220
Oberlin Village 220
Raleigh Planning Commission 220
Pegues, Dr. Albert Witherspoon
Bagley-Daniels-Pegues-Hamlin House
    183
Daniels, Josephus 183
Institute for Deaf, Dumb and Blind
    182
Shaw University 182
Pell, Reverend W.E. 152
Penny Savings Bank 144
Pettiford, Jesse 93
Phoenix Chemical Company 71
Piedmont League Ball Park
Lincoln Court 77
plantations and estates 51, 99, 103, 119
Barringer estate 15, 29, 192
Bledsoe 29, 192
Bledsoe, Moses 15, 176
Cameron Estate 99
Cannon 29, 119
Devereaux 28
Garfield School 60

Gatling 29
Idlewild Plantation 129
Jones, Willie 15
Manly 29, 128
Manly, Governor Charles 15
Mordecai 15, 28
O'Rorke 28
Polk 28
Saunders 29
Smith 29
Watson, J.B.H. 15
Worth, Governor 15
police and sheriff 69, 94
 Crossan, Robert 161
 Dunston, B.H. 122
politics
 Democrats 80
 Lightner, Calvin 180
 Pope, Dr. Manassa 180
 Republicans 80
 Seneca, Bob 180
Pope, Dr. Manassa 182
PTA (Parent Teachers Association)
 Holland, Anna W. 64
Pullen, Howard 72, 131
 ballpark 131
Pullen Park
 Richard Stanhope Pullen 78
Pulliam, R.W. 51

Q

quarry freedmen
 Lane, Major George L. 164
 Williams, Tom 164

R

racism 26, 27, 36, 54, 120
 Chavis Park 78
 Constitution, North Carolina 54
 education 108
 Fayetteville Street 63
 fire companies 71
 fires 136

First Baptist Church 155
 funerals 180
 Gatling, John 207
 housing 151
 Jim Crow 34, 36, 48, 215
 juvenile delinquency 78
 laws passed 21
 library 66
 Lunsford Lane 21
 Nat Turner uprising 21
 Negro jobs 21
 Peace Institute 192
 political punishment 181
 Pullen Park 78
 railroads 148, 149
 Tupper, Dr. Henry M. 191
 water and sewer lines 147
railroads 25, 74, 106, 119, 122, 148,
 192
 baseball 149
 Norfolk Southern Railway 148
 North Carolina Railroad 120
 Raleigh and Gaston Railroad 29,
 148, 149, 151
 Seaboard Airline Railroad 149
 Southern Railroad Company 109
Rainey, Godfrey 202
 Freedmen's Bureau 202
 Lane, Major George L. 202
Raleigh and Gaston Railroad 29, 148,
 149
Raleigh Board of Commissioners
 Harris, James H. 24
 Lockhart, Hardy 24
Raleigh, City of 78, 208
 annexation 100
 Battery Heights 207
 Black mayor 217
 Chavis Park 78
 City Market 35
 fire companies 69, 71, 136
 fire protection 27
 Fourth Ward 27
 Moore Square 35, 36

police 24, 27, 123
Pullen Park 78
Raleigh City Urban Renewal and
    Planning Commission 120, 123,
    124, 125, 152
Second Ward 27
unsanitary conditions 27
Winters, John 213
Raleigh City Urban Renewal and
    Planning Commission
First Congregational Church 125
First Cosmopolitan Baptist Church
    124
Fourth Ward 120
Hayti 120
Macedonia New Life Church 123
Smoky Hollow 152
Raleigh Cooperative Land and
    Building Association 48, 94, 95,
    120, 129
Ashley, S.S. 48
Cotton Place 48
Harris, James H. 48
Hungry Neck 48
Idlewild 48
Oberlin 48
Smith, Reverend J. Brinton 48
St. Petersburg 48
Raleigh Cotton Mill 151
Raleigh Grays 73, 75, 76
Chavis Park 76
Haywood, Charles A. "Doll" 73
McCoy, Red 73
Olmstead, Allen 73
Perry, Willard 73
Taylor 73
Watkins, C.O. 73
Wilder, W.A. "Pete" 75
Williams, Fred 73
Yancey, James 73
Raleigh Institute 26
Raleigh Land and Improvement
    Company 48
Hungry Neck 50

Idlewild 50
Raleigh Real Estate and Trust
    Company 176
Raleigh Tar Heels 73
Harrington, Eulace 73
Paige, "Satchel" 73
Raleigh Theological Institute. See Shaw
    University
Freedmen's Bureau 192
Raleigh Tigers 76, 77
Raleigh Township School Board 54, 62
American Missionary Society 62
Briggs, T.H., Jr. 56
Broughton, Needham B. 56
Brown, Mills 56
Centennial Graded School 56
Crosby School 57
Duggar, Captain John 56
Garfield School 56, 57, 59
Gilbert, M.V. 54
Howell, Superintendent Logan D. 57
Johnson School, the 56, 151, 152
Jones, H.C. 54
Lewis, R.H. 56
McAlpine, Superintendent Andrew
    J. 56
Mordecai, S.F. 56
Moses, Edward P. 56
Oberlin School 56
Primrose, W.S. 56
Reed, Reverend F.L. 56
Root, C.B. 56
Rosenthal, G. 56
Schaffer, Colonel A.W. 54
St. Augustine's College 57
Washington Graded School 56, 62
Whiting, S.W. 56
Reconstruction 17, 34, 95, 102, 128,
    152, 194
baseball teams 72
Battery Heights 212
recreation 72
baseball 74
Chavis Park 79

Depression 75
Reeves, Eliza 163
Rex Hospital 139, 143
  Wyche, Mary Lewis 141
Rhodes, Benjamin 58
  Colored Educational Association of
    North Carolina 58
Rhone, Oliver 58
  Colored Educational Association of
    North Carolina 58
Richard B. Harrison Library 66, 68
  Chavis Heights 67
  Lee, Mollie Huston 66
  St. Agnes Training School for Nurses
    68
  Washington Terrace 67
Richardson, Kittie 98
Rick, Reverend Edward Robbins 142
  St. John's Guild 142
Riddick, Private Samuel 52
Rochester Heights
  advertisements 220, 221
  annexation 220
  boundaries 215
  builder 220
  Cooley, Sidney 218
  Hunter, Willis 218
  Key Homes 218
  Lightner, Calvin 181, 217, 220
  National Historic Register 215
  Neily, Henry 218
  occupations 221
  Peebles, Millard 218
  Phillips Building Corporation 218
  St. Ambrose Episcopal Church 155
  street names 217
  Washington Terrace 218, 224
Rosenwald Foundation 107
Rosenwald, Julius 107
Royster, Dr. Hubert 139
Royster, Dr. W.I. 139
Rush, Bishop Christopher 178
Rush Metropolitan Church 178
  builder 178

Rush, Bishop Christopher 178

S

San Domingo 95
Scales, Tom 149
Scruggs, Dr. Lawson A. 139
Seaboard Airline Railroad 149
Seaboard Railroad 133
Seaboard Station 148
Seawell, Henry 135
Second Baptist Church 25, 59
  education 59
Shaffer, A.W. 123
Shaffer's Addition 123
Shaw, Elijah 192
Shaw University 26, 29, 48, 57, 62, 99,
    116, 130, 164, 182, 183, 184,
    213
  American Baptist Home Mission
    Society of New York 191
  ballpark 194
  Barringer estate 121, 192
  Centennial Graded School 192
  Confederate surrender 192
  Crosby, Henry 60
  entertainment 183
  Estey, Colonel J.J. 194
  Estey Hall 183, 194
  Faculty Row 77, 182, 194
  Freedmen's Bureau 191, 192
  General Assembly 196
  Johnson, E.A. 197
  Law School 197
  Leonard School of Medicine 183,
    196
  Leonard School of Pharmacy 184,
    196
  Leonard Schools of Medicine,
    Pharmacy, Dental and Law 48
  New England Freedmen's Aid Society
    191
  North Carolina Railroad 192
  Peabody Fund 192
  Peace Institute 192

Pegues, Dr. Albert Witherspoon 182
Raleigh Theological Institute 192
Reconstruction 194
Shaw Alumni Field 75
Shaw, Elijah 192
Shaw Hall 192
slavery 17
Smedes, Reverend Albert 134
Smedes, Reverend John Eston Cook 136
Smith, Dr. Albert 95
Smith-Haywood 157, 163
  boundaries 161
  Burns, Tony 161
  Crossan, Robert 161
  Harris, W.N. 163
  Haywood, Dr. Richard 161
  Hodge, Reuben 161
  Lane, Allen 163
  Lane, Major George L. 161
  Lane's Bottom 161
  Marshall, Henry 163
  Reeves, Eliza 163
  Smith, Reverend J. Brinton 161
  South Park/East Raleigh 174
  Whelson, S.N. 163
  Worth, Steve and Winnie 163
Smith, Jerry 137
Smith, Reverend George 125
Smith, Reverend J. Brinton 134, 136, 154, 161
  Oakwood Cemetery 136
  St. Ambrose Episcopal Church 161
  St. Augustine's College 161
Smoky Hollow
  boundaries 148
  Cagle, Connie 149
  Democrats 151
  Dunbar, Jesse 149
  Dunbar, Louis 149
  Fifth Ward 151
  First Baptist Church 151
  Johnson School, the 151
  Norfolk Southern Railway 148

occupations 148
Page, Jimmy 149
Raleigh and Gaston Railroad 148, 151
Raleigh City Urban Renewal and Planning Commission 152
Raleigh Cotton Mill 148, 151
Republicans 151
Scales, Tom 149
Seaboard Station 148
St. Ambrose Episcopal Church 154
St. Augustine's Episcopal Church 151
St. Paul AME Church 151
Society, American Anti-Slavery 21
South Park
  American Veneer and Box Company 176
  Bledsoe, Moses 176
  boundaries 176
  Institute for Deaf, Dumb and Blind 178
  Johnson, E.A. 176
  Raleigh Real Estate and Trust Company 176
  Second Baptist Church 178
  Shaw University 176
  Tupper Memorial Baptist Church 178
South Park/East Raleigh
  Battery Heights 174
  boundaries 174
  Chavis Heights 174
  Cotton Place 174
  National Historic Register 174
  Smith-Haywood 174
  St. Petersburg 174
  Third Ward 174
South Park Hornets 73, 74
  Austin, Elijah 74
  Brevard, Will 74
  Browning, Aaron "Skink" 73
  Jones, Floyd "Deacon" 73
  Shaw, Aaron "Rabbit" 74

Watkins, Joe 73
Wilder, W.A. "Pete" 74
Spencer, H. 202
St. Agnes Hospital. *See* St. Agnes
    Training School for Nurses
St. Agnes Training School for Nurses
    68, 131, 143
  Battle, Dr. Kemp P. 139
  Burgess, Marie 141
  Collins, I.R. 139
  Delany, Dr. Lemuel 139
  description 141
  diploma 141
  Duncan, Dr. Jenny A. 141
  Glendon, Dr. Mary P. 141
  government training program for
      nurses 143
  Hayden, Dr. Catherine P. 141
  Hunter, Sarah 139
  Knox, Dr. Augustus 139
  Ku Klux Klan 141, 143
  Lewis, Dr. Richard H. 139
  McKee, Dr. James 139
  occupations 139
  operations 141
  quarry stone 139
  Rex Hospital 139
  Royster, Dr. Hubert 139
  Royster, Dr. W.I. 139
  Wake County Medical Center 143
  Wyche, Mary Lewis 141
St. Ambrose, Bishop of Milan 134
St. Ambrose Episcopal Church 154
  building moved 155
  Christ Episcopal Church 154
  General Assembly 154, 155
  Harris, James H. 102
  kindergarten 155
  parochial school 154
  Phillips, Mary 155
  Rochester Heights 155
  Smith, Reverend J. Brinton 154
  St. Ambrose School 155
St. Augustine, Bishop of Hippo 134

St. Augustine's College 57, 62, 130,
    131, 134, 144, 154
  Avery, Reverend Charles 134
  Battle, Dr. Kemp P. 134
  Benson, May 139
  Bishop Tuttle Memorial Training
      School 131, 143
  bricks 137
  Camp Russell 134
  Cox, General William 134
  Delany, Bishop Henry 137
  fire 136
  fire companies 136
  Freedmen's Bureau 134
  Freedmen's Commission of Protestant
      Episcopal Church 134
  Hampton Institute 138
  Hayes, Washington 137
  Haywood, William H. 137
  Howard Hall 135
  Hunter, Reverend Aaron 138
  Hunter, Sarah 138, 144
  Jones, Willie 135
  Mason, Reverend Richard S. 134
  Oakwood Cemetery 136
  occupations 135
  Old Fairgrounds 134
  quarry stone 137
  schedule 136
  Seawell, Henry 135
  Smedes, Reverend Albert 134
  Smedes, Reverend John Eston Cook
      136
  Smith, Jerry 137
  Smith, Reverend J. Brinton 134, 136
  St. Agnes Training School for Nurses
      139
  St. Ambrose, Bishop of Milan 134
  St. Augustine, Bishop of Hippo 134
  St. Augustine's Normal School and
      Collegiate Institute 134
  stonemasons 137
  trades 138
  trade school 138

Tuttle Center 131
St. Augustine's Episcopal Church 118,
    151, 154. *See also* St. Ambrose
    Episcopal Church
Stewart, Samuel
    Victor Fire Company 69
St. James AME Church 106
    O'Kelly, Berry 106
St. John's Guild
    hospital 142
St. Mary's College
    St. Augustine's College 134
St. Paul AME Church 151, 152
    African Church, the 152
    Broadie, Reverend George 152
    building moved 152
    Christ Episcopal Church 152
    Edenton Street Church 152
    Freedmen's Convention 152
    Johnson School, the 57
    Lockhart, Hardy 152
    Pell, Reverend W.E. 152
St. Petersburg 48, 163
    boundaries 128
    Manly, Governor Charles 128
    South Park/East Raleigh 174
Stronach, W.C. 157
Swepson, George 48, 51

T

Taylor, Mildred Otey 183
Third Ward
    South Park/East Raleigh 174
Thompson, Dorothy 213
Troops, U.S. Colored
    Third Division of Tenth Corps (Civil
        War) 23
Tupper, Dr. Henry M. 191, 203
    American Baptist Home Mission
        Society of New York 191
    Barringer estate 192
    Freedmen's Bureau 191
    Guion Hotel 191, 203

Leonard Schools of Medicine,
    Pharmacy, Dental and Law 196
Raleigh Theological Institute 192
soldier 191
Tupper Memorial Baptist Church
    203
Tupper Memorial Baptist Church 26,
    203
    Blount Street Baptist Church 203
    Freedmen's Bureau 203
    Guion Hotel 203
    Ligon, John W. 110
    Second Baptist Church 203
    Tupper, Dr. Henry M. 203
Tuskegee Conference 107
Tuttle Center. *See* Bishop Tuttle
    Memorial Training School
Twilight League 74

U

Union Enterprise Company 48
urban renewal 152
    Fourth Ward 123
    Hayti 120
    Smoky Hollow 152
    Southside 120

V

Vance, Governor Zebulon
    Battery Heights 207
    fortification 207
    slavery 207
Victor Fire Company 69, 71
    General Assembly 69
Village of Yesteryear 117
Virginia Union 182
Vogel, Dr. H.C. 53

W

Wake County commissioner
    Caswell, John R. 120
Wake County Medical Center 143
Warrick, Reverend W.M. 156

Warwick, Louisa 58
Warwick, Reverend W.M. 58
  First Baptist Church 58
Washington, Booker T. 110
  National Negro Business League 110
Washington Graded School 56, 120,
    121, 183
  Branch, Professor John 62
  Brewer, Reverend Fisk P. 61
  Capehart, Dr. Lovelace 62
  Davis, Reverend Alfred 62
  First Congregational Church 61
  freedmen's school 61
  Johnson, E.A. 62, 197
  Levister, Professor J.L. 62
Washington High School 63
  Aiken, M.W. 65
  Fayetteville Street 63
  Yeargin, J.W. 63
Washington Terrace 67, 224
Washington, Verde 105
Watson, John W.B. 29
Watson's Addition
  Crosby School 171
  development 171
  Gurley, Milford 171
  Johnson, E.A. 171
  Watson, John W.B. 165
Weathers, Curtis A. 78
Webb, Harold 226
  director of state personnel 226
  Tuskegee airman 226
  Wake County commissioner 226
Webb, Lucille 226
Wheeler, Martha 184
  Shaw University 184
Whelson, S.N. 163
White, Robert 58
  Colored Educational Association of
    North Carolina 58
Wilberforce College 116
Wilder, W.A. "Pete" 74, 75, 76, 77, 79
William, John
  Victor Fire Company 69

Williams, Julia A. 60, 98
Williams, Tom 164
Wilmington-Blount
  Hamlin, Ernestine P. 182
  Shaw University 182
Wilson Temple UMC
  Groom, M.G. 100
Wimberley, Reverend Elias 160
Winston, J.W. 71
Winters, John 213
  Battery Heights 213
  Biltmore Hills 214
  developer 213
  Madonna Acres 213
  Miller, Jerry 214
  North Carolina Utilities Commission
    213
  Raleigh City Council 213
  Senate 213
  UNC Board of Governors 213
Wood, C.H. 105
Works Progress Administration 17
  slave narratives 17, 26
Worth, Steve and Winnie 163
  Worth, Governor 163
Wyche, Mary Lewis 141

Y

Yeargin, J.W. 63

ABOUT THE AUTHOR

Carmen Wimberley Cauthen learned the value of history and family legacy growing up as a child. A Black native of Raleigh, she has always recognized that only some of the stories have been told. While writing the *Journal for the North Carolina House of Representatives*, she realized that truth is many-sided and what is generally shared is only what is comfortable to hear. Her work as a family historian, racial equity advocate and truthteller is helping to raise awareness of the roots of erasure in the Black community's history. Her main desire is to record the truth of all history as opposed to only one side. She reminds us all that "my history, our history" is one of the most valuable lessons we can learn.

Visit us at
www.historypress.com